HEART OF THE CIRCUS

Manna

An Imprint of Edisun Consulting Services
1067, Officers Colony
Anna Nagar West Extension
Chennai – 600101
publishing@iamanauthor.in
www.indie-bookstore.com | www.iamanauthor.in

This book is dedicated to my sons Divyan & Pavan, my reason for staying afloat. Following right behind them are their wives, Rushmitha and Kajal, my power points (as I call them) – always backing me up and standing on the sidelines in the most non-intrusive way and cheering me on.

This book is also for Reuel, Reyah, Aiden and Zeke who will, someday, want to know my story as narrated by me – the story of forgiveness, resilience and strength of your Maachi.

This is also for myriads of virtual and real friends who believed in me and said, "Yes, you can, Manna" – especially for the dynamic group Her Trivandrum (on Facebook) led by Anjali Menon our Captain at the helm, a group that never let me rest until I sat down to pen these stories.

This is for my Appa who left this world some three decades ago. He left me the prayer, "Lord, Bend me, but do not break me". I may have uttered this short prayer a million times in my 66 years.

Above all, it is to my Almighty Lord, for never ever leaving my side at any time.

Foreword

By Johnathan Lee Iverson
(The Last Ringmaster)

Imagine if you will, the privilege of doing what you love with the people you love, making a living while having a life. This was my existence for the better part of my career at Ringling Bros. and Barnum & Bailey as their Ringmaster. My wife worked with the production staff and would eventually ascend to the position of Production Manager where the reins of the multi-million dollar performing arts icon known as The Greatest Show On Earth would be in her hands. Our children, Matthew and Lila, were along for the ride, and not just any ride, but the world's longest privately owned train. The Great American Circus train stretched over a mile long. Aboard it, we crisscrossed the United States in our customized living quarters — two bedrooms, a full bathroom, and living room with a kitchen. There was no better way to see America go by.

It was a city without a zip code and like any city or community there is a culture. Ours was a milieu of people from around the globe with peculiar and spectacular talents, in front of and behind the curtain. It was an institution owned by a family, presented by families, for the enjoyment of families. Believe it or not, our children weren't left to the winds or their whims. They had their society within our society which consisted of a nursery and a school. Some parents, like my wife and I, took full advantage of acquainting our children with the most stellar "PE Teachers" one could dare ask for. Worldclass acrobats from the renowned sports schools of Eastern Europe and Asia were more than anxious to share their hard-earned knowledge of fitness, much to our children's chagrin (at least, in the beginning of their development).

All in all, this was a remarkably charmed existence. Everything seemed to work like clock-work, except when it came to the school. To say I was less than satisfied with our first two-and-a-half years would be kind. I absolutely hated it. Like most parents, providing a quality education for our children was of utmost importance. The assumption when we returned to The Greatest Show On Earth, children in tow, was that their education, at the very least, would be vibrant and unique. What we found was beyond disappointing. Disorder and mediocrity were rampant. Trust between the parents, school staff and show management was non-existent. It was an arduous situation as we watched what we believed to be a most opportune moment in the lives of our children being squandered for lack of sound leadership and, frankly, good teachers. What we endured in those first few years was terrifically subpar – our children had to make do with teachers who seemed hard-pressed to view the world beyond their homogenous existence, which in and of itself is quite the miracle in the midst of a circus community. They had no connection with their students and, thus, they lacked their respect; and children with no real respect can be quite burdensome.

Then suddenly, quite unexpectedly, all was calm. It was the most remarkable thing that made for a most remarkable day. As I ventured down the hallway in one of the many venues for which we were housed in throughout the performance season, and passed the room where school was in session, I found myself wonderfully disturbed, as it was quiet. It was so quiet that I was quite alarmed, and so, I retraced my steps back to the school room. The door was ajar, and for some odd reason, I was a bit apprehensive about sneaking a peek to see what was going on. There she stood – glistening brown skin, neatly cropped hair, with glasses, an easy smile and in full command. Those kids had never ever been that quiet. If I didn't know better, one would think they were transfixed by a sorceress of some kind. With a calm and confident tone, she made her standards pristinely clear. Suddenly, I found myself transfixed as well. Over my shoulder stood our show's general manager beaming with pride and an assured grin as if he'd found the lost Ark of the Covenant. "That's Manna", he whispered gleefully, as if we had all of a sudden been rescued. "Manna? No way, God … that's just too good!" I thought; and sure enough she was good. She was more than good. She was beyond anything we could have hoped for. Suddenly, the parents had an ally and partner in the education of their children, and for a while at least, the management could rest easy knowing we parents weren't going to be breathing down their necks.

Manna was one of us. In circus, you don't play a role. You are your occupation. It isn't merely what you do, it is who you are. Manna was one of us. She was circus, because she didn't merely teach, she was and is an ordained teacher, that is, it is what the great I AM fashioned her to be. In the years we were blessed to have her, I witnessed our children expand. They didn't just learn the required curriculum, they became active and curious thinkers; assignments became missions; and they were now ensconced in a culture of scholastic excellence and an application of that education in real time. It was clear to all concerned and to our benefit that her life experience and proud heritage made her an ideal candidate in the eclectic world of the circus. With her, no child was left behind. It was as if they were granted their own customized education, as she was authentically invested in the wholeness of each child. Who they were and might become further informed what they learned. This was Manna's special kind of magic.

Like the deliverance of sustenance that descended from the heavenlies upon the Hebrew children wandering in the desert enroute to their Promised Land, we too were blessed with our own abundant gift of Manna in the very "Heart of the Circus".

PREFACE

I am glad you are holding this book and are embarking on a journey that may remind you of a fairy tale you have heard as a child. You will not be disappointed, perhaps a tad disbelieving. I have not said anything that is untrue, but may have left out all of the truth. I don't have to tell all the truth all the time, especially if it is going to do more harm than good.

In the 66 years of my life, I have had some highlights – the birth of my sons, welcoming their wives, the birth of grandkids and publishing my first book. All of these are extremely precious. But 8 years of my life, that I spent with an entertainment industry as their on-location-educator, remain unique and unparalleled.

These 8 years have helped me evolve into the person I am now, waking up every morning and falling all over in love with myself.

These 8 years taught me not to look for love and validation elsewhere.

These 8 years erased a lot of lies fed to me, and I have since then re-scripted my life into something real and honest.

These 8 years also helped me chisel out a new perspective of spirituality.

These 8 years allowed me to see friends and family as humans first and then as people playing different roles.

Contents Inside

Introduction

One of the movies that I watched on a loop in the '90s was The Titanic. While Leonardo Di Capri and Kate Winslet put in a splendorous act as Jack and Rose, what caught my romantic side was the aged Rose – how she kept the diamond "Heart of the Ocean" with her all those years. It was only hers and no one was privy to it. The unsinkable sank, Jack died; Rose moved on. In the midst of it all, the diamond survived and lived to tell the story of love and passion.

The Greatest Show goes on. Things change, friends don't.

Age is respected, youth is celebrated.

People meet for brief periods but remain friends forever.

At the show, your problem is mine, and mine yours, and

nothing is unresolved.

In the midst of the spectacular show, neither religion, sex nor

marital status matter.

You are accepted for who you are. For the first time I felt

counted, valued.

"Could there be a Heaven on Earth?" I have often wondered.

Unnoticed but mightily, lay the Heart of the Circus ...

A one-room school, all my students and I would always

be the "Heart of the Circus".

CHAPTER 1

"My name is Manna", I replied to someone who asked what my name was. "Who named you 'Manna'" was the next question. "I named myself", I answered a little surprised. She seemed puzzled as much as I looked foolish giving that answer. I knew I had to explain. This was my version of my naming ceremony. I was baptized and given my paternal mother's name, which was Maria. Today, Maria sounds chic, but those days it sounded too plain. Anyway, I loved it because my father, ever since I remember, called me Maria. That's probably what registered first in my brain. This tiny little organ while taking in the information did not know that it will have to make room for billions of other information that was to follow.

When people asked me as a little girl, hardly two years, what my name was, I always said, "Marnia". The little baby way of saying Maria. I always got the response, "Oh! Manna! That's a wonderful name". Seeing the joy and gleam in the other person's eyes, I decided it was better to be called Manna than Maria. Thus, I became Manna, not because anyone thought I was special, or a gift from God, but people just looked at me and gave me that name, no matter how hard I tried to tell them it was Maria. Was there a reason why my tongue wouldn't roll the "R" enough to remain Maria? Was there a reason why "Manna" stuck as my name? Wherever I went, everyone seemed to spend more than a minute talking about "Manna" as soon as I introduced myself.

I loved the attention when I was young and later when I was growing up too. Much later it became inconvenient, for no one would easily forget it, and it was catchy and poetic, so it was used both creatively and destructively. Many said I was like the Manna from heaven, a blessing. Others said I was there for anyone to pick, easily available. And I knew both of these were not true. I was just an ordinary woman, with an extraordinary womanhood!

I was born into a conservative family. Born with a destiny so big that I am sure if my parents had had a glimpse of what was to happen, they would have been petrified. Fortunately, that didn't happen and each of them wove their own dreams and expectations of what they envisaged as my life. Since both their dreams did not concur, I grew up with mixed messages and images. I was raised with a long list of what I could do and couldn't do. The couldn't-do list was way longer than the can-do list, as family and society felt they had to have a say in my life. I was trained as a dog would be trained, to just obey. The difference was this obedience fetched no treats but disobedience fetched punishments. I kept obeying because every instruction was followed by a threat of how miserable my life would be if I didn't obey, how the world would see me as a wayward, headstrong lady, and how I would be the least sought in the marriage market. The scariest of them was how I would grow old, grey and toothless and still be waiting only to be rejected over and over. Try this on your little girl and see how she turns out!

As I grew up with the constant fear of rejection, I ended up learning to please everyone. I ended up wanting to cling on to any attention I would get, albeit it was negative or abusive. I tended to think it will at least not make me alone, old, grey and toothless. I was afraid of being invisible. Soon people around me, starting from within the family, began perceiving me as everyone's favourite. Gradually I was getting a lot of attention because I never said no, or ever stood up for myself. I was no threat to anyone. I talked loudly and profusely. I sounded smart and strong. But the icy hands of fear were wrapped around my heart at all times. I laughed more and made friends with no discretion. I was called friendly, bold, even arrogant. In reality, the "real me" inside was dying and begging for attention every single moment.

The first man I adored and loved implicitly – I must mention him. My life has never been complete without him. It never will be either. He was tall, well-built, strong, a smile encompassing all, unbiased, open. He was a go-getter, a winner all the way. He stuck to his guns no matter what. Above all, he doted on this wide-eyed, curly haired cherubic daughter. He lavished her with love and affection and wove a web of security around her, so strong and steadfast, yet in certain ways tragically unrealistic. He was also the first one to disappoint me. My father!

To me, as a little girl, all men were harmless, doting and loving, like my adorable father. This tenet was the cause of all disaster that was to ensue, as time beat me to it. To me, he was infallible. After several decades of life, I am yet to find someone on par or even close to him. This could also be an act of the mind to buffer me from the bitterness and hatred against the world that was welling up inside me. His memory is like a splash one takes after a walk on a hot day. His memory is also a reminder that the entire world isn't after all a bad place to live in.

In my agony and disappointment, I trudged on with the hope of finding someone who was like my father, or at least aspired to attain that status. Am I angry that he was not honest with me? Am I frustrated that he has been proved wrong? Am I hurt that I have probably been led to live a myth? Do I doubt my perception now? These questions flit in and out of my mind in my most vulnerable moments.

He encouraged me to be really strong, and he told me occasionally that it was OK to think independently. He showed me, not consistently but in spurts, what I could really be. Along with these empowering moments also came a restrain to not achieve it. Very confusing indeed! It seemed like he was afraid to let me become who I was meant to be. But I had made a mental note and tucked it away in a teeny tiny corner of my mind to try it out some day. And that has been my survival tactic.

Therefore, from choosing my career path to my life partner, I just remained obedient. I became obedient to anyone who showed me a little kindness, or gave me a little attention. I remember times when I instinctively didn't like or agree with someone but didn't do anything about it for fear of rejection. I allowed them to use me, abuse me or walk over me. I just obeyed – like a dog that's trained. The dog's sole objective is to please the trainer and collect treats. Was my childhood good? Yes, for the most part. Was I bullied? I don't know. Maybe, some of the demands bordered on bullying. I didn't know these things when I was growing up with a feeling of inadequacy. I forgave the bully and gave leeway to the perpetrator. I had become easily forgiving. Every time I felt like I wanted to say no, I would think of growing old, grey, toothless and alone. That was the scariest thing for me, to grow old ALONE. So, I became easily affable. I had to find a partner and those days the only approved partnership was marriage. Those days bullying was sugar-coated as friendly teasing; protesting meant I was not a sport according to my peers, and when I stood up for myself, I was belligerent according to the significant adults in my life. Feigning amenability meant I was a "good girl". All the while deep inside me, the dependable inner voice kept telling me I was wrong. I did not listen to it. Although it seemed rational, it also smelt of isolation.

As I am writing this, I am making a mental audit. I love arithmetic. My brain every now and then does this weird thing. It calculates the percentage of random things. It takes away boredom. For instance, if I am in church and the preacher rambles on about judgements, or manipulates the mind of people in attendance to prove their guilt, I look around and count how many people are wearing white and then calculate the percentage of people wearing white that day. If the congregation offers me enough variety, then I calculate the percentage for all the different colours. I have digressed.

Yesterday I did a little calculation because I had just done celebrating my 66th birthday. What percentage of my life had I spent looking for approval and validation? I came with a staggering 67%. I sat staring at the number. If, say, I lived to be 75 (an optimistic estimate), I would have spent more than half my lifetime pleasing others. Hold that thought.

Recently, by some stroke of the universe, there was a burst of attention that came my way without my seeking it. By way of media! Mostly from random people who thought my life was worth the narration. Several interviews and many opportunities to tell my story, without interruption, opened my eyes to a lot of insights into myself. One question was, "At what point in your life did you know you had to throw your pain and losses behind you and move forward?" This was a difficult one. I had to think. It was then that I realized there was no one date or moment. It just happened.

I just knew at one point in my life I couldn't take it anymore. The swirling restlessness inside me was at a point of eruption. That is when I clawed back. I transitioned from being Jekyll to Hyde. Reckless and self-destructive at times. Abrasive and aggressive in my words and actions. I didn't care for myself anymore and therefore didn't care for others either. I was not afraid of being alone anymore. I looked forward to getting old. But I also knew I had to live before I started getting old. This realization, I guess, was when I decided I needed to turn from being a victim to a victor. That was the moment I realized that the choice to be a victim or victor lay within me.

CHAPTER 2

The year I turned 60 something shook me. I lived alone and had seen a lot of peers celebrate their 60th with such grandeur. I knew if I didn't do something about celebrating, I would have just another day go by with a few greetings on WhatsApp and Facebook and a few phone calls. I wanted more. So, I got into the planning and sought the help of a few I considered important in my life. Very soon things began to fall into place. My 60th was indeed a celebration.

The planning, the preparing, the excitement was all going as per the blueprint. Friends poured in their ideas and everything seemed to go well.

It was in the midst of my planning with a good friend that something dropped like a bomb shell. I laughed at it but she wouldn't let it go as something trivial. She noticed an unusual and annoying mannerism in me. I would rub hard on my left breast every now and then. After a couple of times, she joked about it. That's when I said I had been having a niggling pain, and when I rubbed it, it went away. She immediately took that seriously and the next day coaxed me into getting a mammogram done. That was going to be the day I would see the end of the finish line in my mind. I realized it may be closer than I thought. You know how in situations like this, most of the time, the reel plays backwards? I saw myself lying in a coffin, random people shedding tears, and then the hospital, the gibberish from doctors, the shock and uncertainty, the fuss and then the mammogram. My friend, thank God, had more sense than me, and her head was screwed the right way on her shoulder. Long story short, I had a surgery and a benign tumour was removed. It left a hole in my left breast. I even now refer to it as my emptiness. It was something to make me stop and take toll of my life. This reel, in real life, played from mammogram to doctors, to surgery and stopped. A lease on life. I knew then that my life was not going to be over so fast and so easily. I started looking for a purpose. Pleasing others and looking for validation were definitely not on the list.

Many years of my life went worrying about others. Worrying about keeping them comfortable, about not hurting them. Even if I was hurting or miserable, I discounted my fears and sadness. My pain was not as important as the pain of others. This way of life was not rewarding. It never would be, as I was to realize later, that if I did not take care of myself, I would soon become a hollow shell.

I would not believe it, because these were not the messages I grew up with. The childhood messages were embedded very deep into my mind and had come from people who I looked up to, or from people who threw me crumbs of attention. This made the struggle to unlearn and relearn real. There are a lot of people who live their entire life in this manner, no escape or redemption. I finally chose a road. Not a road less travelled, I broke a path of my own, cutting down brambles as I moved forward. I became a path breaker. I broke loose, like a stallion breaking loose of its unwilling tether and running aimlessly into the wild. What I could taste was not fear or confusion but the pure joy of freedom. That's the best analogy that keeps coming to my mind over and over. I will stick to it. Armed with the one and only thought of wanting to breathe, like a diver coming up to get air, I made up my mind to go far away and just survive. I had no plan, no vision, no goal. Except, maybe, to just survive.

CHAPTER 3

Seventeen years later and an impressive collection of experiences in my heart, I was now ready to return home, to the land of my birth. I unloaded my luggage from the car and walked into Logan International Airport, Boston, with my heart pounding. I went through the normal procedures of checking in my luggage, collecting my boarding pass, going through immigration. I winced as they stamped my passport with the exit seal. It was official I was bidding adieu to US of America almost 12 years later. As I walked towards the gate I kept wondering if I should just go back. Would they let me out? How does that work? Unrealistic thoughts fighting reality ... As I reached the gate, I looked for a seat away from the rest of the passengers and sat down. I found a seat close to the gate, facing the runway. I sat there watching the planes take off and land, I thought, "they are like me" – soaring and coming down to earth just like the past 17 years of my life since I left my own country. One minute I am up, next down. It then dawned on me that I was finally going back home from my self-imposed exile. I felt like there the soaring may never happen, and even if it did, the landing would be more of a crash. Seventeen long years. Fulfilled, content, yet a dull ache. Leaving behind the country that sustained me and helped me re-define myself, I was carrying a lot of great memories, interlaced with heartache and nostalgia. I could always get back, I consoled myself. I looked at my watch. An hour and a half more left for boarding. I look around me - a last glimpse of the US of America. "No", I mumbled aloud, "I need to get back home", I told myself. "It was time".

Time to get back:

To my children and grand-children

To friends

To the aromatic food

To judgements

To alienation

To inquisitions

To the familiar place where I grew up, where both love and hostility awaited me

I sat up straight when I heard the announcement to board the flight. And told myself, "Bring it on".

I found my seat and slowly settled down. It was going to be a long flight to Frankfurt. I had a window seat. The seat next to me was empty. I had prayed it to be so. But soon it was occupied by a lady who was on her cell phone. I involuntarily listened to her conversation. Oh! A micro-manager. She was giving instructions to her husband on feeding the dog, closing the garage door, checking the back door every night, taking the kid to a birthday party ... I turned away smiling to myself. He was not going to do any of these things. All she would get was a series of "Yes, dear" in the most obedient tone. Finally, she was asked to switch off her phone. She did so. Then pulls it out one more time and sent one last message. My side glance read the words, "I love you, honey". I turned towards the window and smiled again. The compulsive behaviour of looking for reassurance.

As the crew got ready with last minute checks, the lady turned to me and asked, "Vacation?"

I said, "No, I'm going home".

"Right. For a break?" she persisted.

"No, I'm not coming back", I replied a tad rudely.

Not deterred by my tone, the stranger still went on to ask me a lot of questions. Basically, by the end of it, and half way to Frankfurt, I realized I was doing the right thing. Talking to her was free therapy.

Meals were served and we ate in silence. I closed my eyes and decided to take a nap. One way to stop the lady from starting inquisition #2.

An announcement woke me up telling us we were close to Frankfurt. What I heard was, "You are closer to home". Flashes of my 17-year-old and 21-year-old sons waiting at the airport set my heart pounding again. My babies. I realized they were not 17 and 21. They were 26 and 30 now. Both married. Tears welled up in my eyes. And despite my efforts, it rolled down. Was it tears of joy at the thought I was going to them? Or was it the pain of guilt for not being there for them? Perhaps a little of both.

I was again at the gate this time in European soil. I was waiting expectantly to board the big silver bird that was taking me home. My home of the past couple of decades seemed so far away. Behind me. Yes. I needed to put it behind me.

Now along with the excitement of seeing my sons after a long time, and seeing my grandson for the first time, there was also the fear of facing the very community I grew up in.

To them:

I was the wayward one.

I was the one with no aim.

I was the black sheep of the family.

I was the one to face the harsh reality that the rest of my journey was going to be a solo ride. They were all waiting to pick up from 16 years ago, while I had moved on a lot ahead, evolved into a woman with an obtrusive strength behind the smile that lit up my eyes.

This battle was going to be pretty much one with the same theme "Survival" – except that it was going to be on my own soil and therefore that much more difficult.

I did a little shopping at the duty-free shops and then I was all set to begin the second and final leg of my journey.

I was again at a window seat on the big silver bird that was taking me home. I pulled out my phone and saw a message from my friend in Boston.

"Hey, in Frankfurt?"

"Yes. Waiting for take-off".

She then called me.

"Have a safe trip. Message me when you reach Madras. (She never said Chennai.)"

"I will (I choked). I am scared (I whispered)".

"You got this girl! It's going to be a piece of cake for you after what you have gone through here. I will be coming soon to visit you. You are too strong for the Indian soil to break you".

"Bye Vimmi. And hey, thanks for everything".

I spent the last leg of my journey in reading, listening to music and watching an in-flight movie. I was so glad that I could watch Erin Brockovich just before I got off to land on my soil. That is my go-to movie when I want to feel that extra nudge inside to spur me on. My home of the past decades seemed so far away - clear but somewhere behind me. Yes. I put it behind me. It simply meant I go forward only.

I went back to my introspection.

If it wasn't for all the humiliation, I would never have done what I did exactly 24 years ago. Not only flown out to the land where many dreams have come true, but also the land where my own people taught me that a leopard doesn't change its spots. It also taught me no one is your friend, especially if you have a broken marriage. The humiliation from people I thought were friends ... The people who had once said they would support me, who turned away ... The humiliation that left me hollow of dignity and self-respect ... However, I was not one to be broken. And that pluck is what enforced the thought of detachment in me. "Detach yourself in order to gain a perspective of what you want to be". That inner voice seemed to say, "Clear your mind"!

CHAPTER 4

Every attempt to detach myself from the known and familiar only took me to a state of fear and anxiety and defeat. I felt like a hamster on a Ferris wheel. Always running but reaching nowhere.

These thoughts petered out as the cheerful voice came over to announce the descent into Chennai. I craned my neck to catch my first glimpse of Chennai in almost two decades – the town where I grew up, the town where I graduated from, the town that held a lot of memories and the city that held friends, who after decades were still there, waiting to pick up the threads from where we had dropped it. I could see nothing except miles of clouds like cotton candy. My heart raced faster than the speed of the plane. I would be seeing my children. Even touching them. I won't be able to cradle them in my arms now. They were grown married men. I could certainly hug them. I knew I was going to embarrass them with my weeping. Tears flowed and I had no control over them. It was sadness at having missed them, tears of joy at being able to return to them, and tears for all that was said, unsaid, done and undone. Unashamedly I allowed the tears to flow. My fellow passenger looked at me in dismay and asked, "Are you alright?" I was almost hyperventilating. "Oh! These?" I said as I pointed to my face and sheepishly said. "These are tears of joy that I have to drain out of my tear ducts before I see my sons or they are going to be soaked in it", I replied with an embarrassing smile. I had no time to explain myself further to the fellow passenger. I was rehearsing my lines of greeting for each of my sons. I had a dozen different scenarios playing in my mind about the way in which I would greet them. None seemed to be adequate. Finally, the plane emerged from those clouds and I glanced at Chennai again, after years. The place I loved. Chennai. My Madras. As I have said before, Chennai is a city, while Madras is an emotion. To this day when I go somewhere and return, I feel like the city hugs me. To me it holds the people I loved, the people I lived for, the school that educated me, the college that enlightened me, the friends that supported me. Before I got intoxicated with euphoria, I came down to earth along with the plane … This place could also tear me apart. I shuddered at the thought. The very people because of whom I had to run away were still there. While I had evolved into a different being, it was not necessary that they would have too. This was a scary situation for me. But then, I told myself, "You have already been on an anvil and have passed through the refiner's fire. You've got this!"

Getting off the plane, and setting foot on Indian soil, was indeed a hallowed moment. I closed my eyes and took a long deep breath … Two decades later that smell was still there. That distinct smell of this city. The name may have changed from Madras to Chennai, the city may have grown, the people may have aged, but the intensity of the emotion remained the same. I smiled and walked towards the immigration with a new confidence brought on by the familiar smell of Chennai. The rest of the things went by as if in a dream. I had two sets of baggage – one on the trolley I was pushing, the other in my heart, both Indian and foreign.

Onward, forward, a foot at a time, I drew closer to the exit. A throng of people were waiting to receive their families and friends. Their expressions showed anticipation, joy, tension, expectation, fear, doubt. That tangible array of emotions sent a deep sense of comfort in me. I am in the land where people are alive and real. No one tries to hide their feelings. Somewhere in that crowd would be my sons too. What emotion would I see on their faces? What do they look like, have they become taller, stouter? My eyes were brimming with tears. I just kept walking almost blindly …; they must find me. It was too much for me to search for them in the crowd. Then I saw him. My baby. Tall, slender, handsome. Gone was the face of the high-school boy. Very different from the high-school boy who stood before the microphone giving his final speech as the head boy of the school. He was now a young man. A French beard, a maturity on his face, but the same kind eyes. The same charming smile. I couldn't take a step forward. Suddenly I felt my feet would give way. He came towards me and I held him tight in my arms, tears flowing. He took the cart from me and he started pushing it. Typical of all young men, he felt embarrassed not just at my tears but at the tumultuous emotions inside him. I was his mother and I was seeing him, touching him, hugging him after almost 8 years. How do you think I should have reacted? What I really wanted to do was bawl loudly, scream until all the pain trapped inside me would come out. I didn't. I held back once more. This was only one of my heartbeats. Where was the other one? As I looked once more towards the throng of people, I asked him, "Where is your brother? Didn't he come?" He didn't answer, but with a grin looked over my shoulder. I felt a tiny tap on my shoulder. I turned around and there stood my first born, a big grin on his face – all the while watching the melodramatic reunion of mama and the younger one. He had the most guarded expression all the time. But his eyes were always a give-away. The kindest eyes you can ever see. He has a way of looking deep into your soul. I now lost control and started crying noisily. Both boys were giggling … each whispering, "Amma! Stop the drama! At least wait until you are in the car. Haven't you learnt to cry in soft sniffles from the US of America!"

Their teasing comments went on incessantly, trying to ease the situation.

I now laughed with them. My heart felt like it would burst with an overwhelming feeling of love. These two had an innate ability to be comedians and could wipe all my sadness in a jiffy. I wiped my eyes and when my eyes were clear, I saw all the people watching this drama unfold before their eyes. Some were grinning, others looking with compassion, some were even seen wiping a tear away. I told you Madras was an emotion! Everyone joined in everyone's pain and joy.

CHAPTER 5

It took me a week to settle down and get over my jet lag. Also, to accept the sad fact that I was not going back ever … to the place that helped me regain my self-worth. Most evenings were spent together with the sons and their wives and my grandson. A new kind of experience. Sons looked at me quizzically every now and then. Daughters-in-law had a lot of questions. My two-year-old grandson had no questions, he just wanted to be around me. The thing I love most about children … they just accept you the way you are. They are refreshing the way they are. Then we adults enter into their lives to teach them to be "proper".

I was sitting on the balcony and sipping my coffee one morning, when my daughter-in-law joined me.

She: What are you thinking, ma?

Me: I can't believe I am here.

She: Do you miss being in the US?

Me: Yes of course I do. (I smiled). But I am glad I am back.

She was quiet for a minute and then asked me softly,

"Was there no other way? I know these years have been very tough for you".

I took a moment to answer.

Me: Perhaps, but at that point I had to get away. I felt like a deer that was being chased by hounds. I feared for my life, not in a literal sense, but in the way most women die from the inside. Little by little. I was not ready to give up.

She reached out and gently pressed my hand and asked, "How did you go to the US?"

*Me: That was a miracle. Honestly another of my impulsive decisions to grab the lemons and make lemonades. That's all it was. It was 2001 October. If you know the history, you would think I was crazy. A lot of my friends thought so too. I agree. It was a month after the attack on the Twin Towers. No one, I mean **no one** was getting their visa. But I found it very difficult to continue in Kuwait, especially after my younger son left. So, after many discussions in the staff room with colleagues (mostly Americans), I was impelled to go to US at least for a vacation. "Go test the waters" was the consensus in the staff room. Most of my colleagues saw me as someone not suited for Indian life. I think it was my independence and guts, which to them was unlike any other Indian woman they had met. With their rallying and my spirit of adventure, I decided to do just that. My thought was, "What do I stand to lose". Things couldn't get worse. It could only get better.*

And if things didn't work out, I could always return to India. This, I prayed, was going to be a sign if I should go West or East. It was like tossing a coin – applying for visa being the coin.

So, one fine day, I reached the US Embassy in Kuwait. There was a long line of people waiting. I saw the line and wanted to turn back. But decided to give God a chance. At that point in time, it was like what some wise person had said, "When in doubt, toss a coin. When it is in the air, your heart will whisper the answer".

My daughter-in-law sat riveted. I sat lost in thought to the events that transpired that day at the embassy. My heart kept whispering, "You must go". It was all very well for the heart to say that. The American embassy held my fate. I continued …

There were about five people ahead of me – all Kuwaitis. I was sure they would all get their visas, and while the positive drift was on, I hoped I would get a piggy-back ride in that drift. But all the five before me were rejected. The angry way in which they walked out told me that. By the time there were just two people ahead of me, I wanted to walk out. My heart sank. I had a friend with me. I told her, "Let's get out of here. I don't want a stamp on my passport saying I've been rejected". But she forced me to stay on. "We will know one way or the other", she said. I remembered the coin toss analogy. Except that now the coin was in the air and I wanted it to be a "yes".

My token number was called and I walked up to the window and there sat a woman with no expression whatsoever on her face. I said a cheerful, "Good Morning", eliciting no response.

She looked at me and asked, "So why do you want to go to the US?" I said, "Over the years, I have virtually watched the ball drop for New Years' in Times Square. This year I want to be there; it is on my bucket list. I have two weeks of winter break and want to return when school opens".

She took the stamp and put that coveted seal on my passport. I couldn't believe my eyes. Now it was my turn to give the expressionless response. I mumbled an unemotional "Thank you" and walked out, head bent down. My friend got up from her seat and came and put her arms around me and said, "It's ok. It is not meant to be". I "hmmed" and kept walking through the waiting lounge. We were still in the embassy premises. She walked silently next to me, probably regretting she had forced me to stay on. As we left the building and entered the parking lot, I turned to her and gave her a hug and said, "I got it". She grabbed my passport and opened it and looked at the stamp incredulously and let out her favourite expletive, *%#*!! The coin had come down in my favour. It was a sign!

Thus began my preparation to go in December. Warm clothes were on top of my list. I called my BFF in Boston and told her I was coming. And we began to plan for Christmas and New Year.

CHAPTER 6

My first trip to the US was not without hiccups. I was travelling from Kuwait to Boston via London. A colleague of mine was sending her 7-year-old daughter with me to London. She was an unaccompanied passenger but my colleague felt comforted that the little girl would have me for company. I set off on my Great Christmas Vacation with the 7-year-old in tow. We went through immigration, got both our passports stamped and headed towards the gate. The British Airways staff felt relaxed knowing someone else was doing their job. We sat near our gate, waiting to board. I played tic-tac-toe, dots and crosses, hangman and whiled away time. Hot meals were served as soon as the plane took off, and soon, we settled down for a nap. In about 5 hours, we were getting ready to land in London Heathrow Airport. The flight attendant told me that she would take the little girl through immigration and customs and hand her over to her grandparents. The 7-year-old and I parted ways and I had just 45 minutes to board my next flight. I was fascinated by the Heathrow Airport with its ostentatious shops, cafes and thousands of people. I knew I had no time to shop. I walked slowly like a tourist on a sight-seeing trip. A little later when I looked at the time, I had just 15 minutes. Now I started to walk fast and sometimes run, dragging my roll-on suitcase in one hand and my handbag in the other. As I neared the gate, I heard the BA staff shout out "Are you Mary?" I waved my hand as I was out of breath. She said "Hurry! We are closing the gate". I apologized profusely and handed her my boarding pass which I had collected at Kuwait itself. She took that and said, "May I see your passport please?" She was a sweet, gentle young lady. I said, "Sure", and dug into my handbag. (I hate these handbags with several pockets.) I had tooth brush, hair brush, hand towel, pens, notepad, lipstick, a half-opened packet of cookies, half a bottle of orange juice, a lot of muck … but no passport. The airline staff waited patiently and seeing a slight panic told me to look calmly. I emptied all of the contents on to the chair nearby, and all these things fell out but not the passport. Whatever happened to it! I felt my heart pounding in my ears, my stomach felt squeamish. My knees felt all wobbly and weak. I looked at the lady helplessly and said, "I can't find my passport". Here I am running away from all things scary and insecure, and I find myself in a country where I expected to be for 45 minutes, but now for over an hour, and with no ID proof. And did I tell you, it was less than a year after the Twin Towers were hit. Need I say more. The lady walked away from me and spoke on her radio briefly. She then walked back to me and said, "Ma'am, we've got to unload your luggage and let the flight go. It's already late". I gathered all the stuff and threw it back into my hand bag. I could feel tears fill my eyes. Is this another story like that of Jonah and the whale? Will I be thrown back on my land? Is that where I am supposed to be? The staff showed me a corner seat, close to her desk, and told me I had to sit there and couldn't leave as I had no ID on me. I looked around and found that about 50 feet away, there stood a circle of men and women, some in uniform and some in regular clothes. That's when I realized the gravity of the situation. Here I am on a foreign soil with no ID and at a time when security was on high alert on terrorism. It had been just 9 months since the terrorist attack on the US soil. There was nothing I could do. I closed my eyes shut imagining that when I opened my eyes again, it would all just go away. But it didn't.

I took a few deep breaths and tried to relax. The same sweet lady came to me and said, "Please try to think if you had taken the passport out on the plane". She really wanted to help. I answered feebly, "No". I leaned back on the seat, closed my eyes and tried to replay my trip. Then I remembered that I had taken my hair brush out just before landing at London. Maybe I had dropped the passport in the process on the plane. I got up from my seat to walk up to her desk and the whole team of cops/secret services moved in unison and said, "Please do not leave your seat!" Geez! Did I just pee in my pants a bit? I sat back in my seat. The lady walked up to me and maintaining a safe distance asked me what I wanted to say. I told her that I may have dropped the passport while pulling out my hair brush. She immediately got on the radio with the airlines and she was told that they had done cleaning the plane and no one had handed over any passport. I had a few minutes of hope to hold on to, which was like coming out of the water for a deep breath. Although my heart was sinking, I did not give up hope or become nervous. I continued replaying the scene in my mind. This was done dispassionately, unemotionally. I went all the way back to the Kuwait airport. I remember us saying our goodbyes to the little girl's mom, the baggage check-in, the immigration officer who stamped our passports the last place where we both would need the passport to go through. I also remember thinking, I better put the kid's passport into her back-pack. But then … I don't remember putting mine into *my* handbag. I noticed I was not breathing. I was holding my breath. I think at that point I knew what I had done. Before I could call the airline staff over, I replayed the scene once more in my head. Yes! I may have put my passport into the child's back-pack along with her passport. Oh! God! I knew I was doomed. How will I get it back? I did not have any details of the child's grandparents. No address or phone number. I closed my eyes once more for a second and prayed, "Lord not my will but yours be done". I signalled to the staff again. I told her with conviction what I had done. She was so happy, happier than me and immediately asked me for the contact of the grandparents. I looked her straight in the eye and said, "I don't have it. The airlines should have it, as the child was an unaccompanied minor". She gave me a look which may have been, "You must make this hard for me, mustn't you? "Then she was on the phone making a few calls while I sat there holding on to my last straw. I did not even want to imagine what would happen if the passport was not in the child's back-pack or the grandparents had gone away to some holiday destination with the grandchild. Being in a situation as critical as that and trying not to panic is agony. A few minutes later, the lady came to me and said that no one was picking the phone. I pleaded with her to keep trying. I feigned confidence and said, "They may be living far away from the airport and they must be still getting home". She kept trying. Finally, they picked the phone. She asked a few questions about their ID and then asked them to check the back-pack of the kid. The next thing I knew this airline staff let out a cry, "Yes! They do have your passport". The security personnel on the ground and the airline staff all got busy talking to sort this out. I let the tears flow, not before thanking the good Lord for His mercy. It was a good 15 minutes, which of course seemed like 15 hours. The lady came up to me and said,

"We have sent one of our own staff to go pick up your passport from them. They live 40 miles out. That's an 80-mile trip to and fro. I am hoping you can take the late-night flight. Let me book you on it". I looked with gratitude at her wordlessly. She was a patient kind soul. Wherever she is, I always pray that she is blessed immensely. The security team had now dwindled to a couple. They seemed relaxed and some even gave me a smile. It definitely was not a sympathetic smile; it was more of amusement …, like I had given them entertainment for the day. I also asked her if she could call a number in Boston and inform my friend that I had missed the flight. No details. She obliged. By now, I was exhausted. I needed something to eat and drink and also use the restroom. But they wouldn't let me walk around without an ID on me. But even there I was given an exception. I was told to use the restroom which the airline staff could see from her post, and as for coffee and sandwich, she got it for me. Angels everywhere, all the time.

The rest of the trip was uneventful. Except when I reached Boston, my friend reprimanded me for wasting time walking to the next gate and missing my flight. She assumed my laid-back attitude would have caused it. We were at the baggage claim and I said calmly, "I lost my passport". She laughed and looked at me. Then she saw my face and said, "What?" I told her I would tell her more on reaching home. She stopped at a restaurant along the way and ordered some refreshing drinks and some food and we talked. She looked stricken. Her eyes too had tears. She is the only one who would understand me and my idiosyncrasies. "You are here now. Let's get some food in and go home".

A long silence and my daughter-in-law said, "I cannot even begin to imagine what you went through. And here we are thinking, you just glided gracefully into the US".

"I had got a taste of the US of A in December. I loved it. When I took the flight back on the 2nd of January, I was still in a daze, like I had been to a fairy land", I continued talking to my daughter-in-law, after I got myself a drink of ice-cold water.

My daughter-in-law smiled. She had a look of both belief and disbelief on her face. I sat silently and listened to my inner voice. It was the trundling of the train. I knew it would be a while before I got that out of my head.

After I returned from the vacation, all my friends at work in Kuwait were waiting to hear about my trip. Most of them were Americans, as it was an International School. They were all happy that I was stoked and full of praise for their country. I felt even more special because there were some Americans who had not seen the ball drop for New Year's. I was very surprised and couldn't believe that someone who lived in that country had not seen the big New Year's event in New York. But then, neither have I seen the Taj Mahal!!

The voice of my daughter-in-law intruded into my

thoughts, "Then how did you end up there for 12 years???"

Me: I returned after my dream vacation in January. Six months went by and the summer holidays came. My travel itch began again. (I smiled) I decided to go back for a better look at the US. Since I had only a single-entry visa, I decided to apply again. I felt more confident and even a bit cocky. I went for my visa entry, and this time I got a 10-year multiple entry visa. This time my answer to the consular officer was, "I loved what I saw on my last visit and now I want to see the Grand Canyon, Niagara Falls and The Statue of Liberty". In reality, I never got to see the Grand Canyon and Niagara Falls but spent days in Vegas and The Smithsonian Museum.

She: "Wow!"

That's the only word she could say.

Me: Yes, Wow indeed! This time I had two months of summer break to spend there. I could look around a bit. I decided to find a place of my own and choose a new place. I chose the capital city as my online search took me to a rental with an Indian widow in McLean – a suburban area of the Fairfax County in Virginia. My neighbour was Colin Powell, The United States Secretary of State. Go figure! I smiled at my own naivety. I made a choice, sitting in Kuwait and randomly picking a place, just because it was a place owned by an Indian widow. My daughter-in-law sat with her mouth agape. It was not something I could really afford. But how would I know?

There were friends and family but I knew no one who would have me. Our community whether in India or the US could only see me as the woman who left her husband and abandoned her children! My friend in Boston was always there, but I did not want to impose myself on her. My social life was limited. I barely went out. One thing I did was buy a metro pass and crisscrossed across Washington DC. In a short time, I knew which metro line to use to get from one place to the other. I also soon found stations where they had good food courts. Living in DC and renting my own room gave me breathing space. Now it was June and a lesson I learned: "What you taste of a country during the holidays is not what really happens in that country on regular days". On regular days, life happens, birth, death, sickness, accidents, job losses, employment, all mundane things. During my first visit in December, I loved the festivity; I loved the spirit of cheer; there was a feeling of goodwill and kindness everywhere. I was overwhelmed by what I saw for real, in person, and what I had been watching virtually, over many years. Such a blessed country. The New Year's ball drop was the last thing I had experienced in the US of A, in that short visit.

My daughter-in-law showed signs of restlessness and I realized it best to stop the narration. So, I changed gears.

Me: What are we going to have for lunch?

She: Really not my department. He (husband) does most of it.

Me: Oh! Let me whip something up. Let's see what we got here.

I walked to the kitchen, rummaged through the refrigerator and came up with some things and quickly made some easy lunch. I am a good cook and a creative one at that. So that was a no-brainer. I then sat down to cool off; the humidity and heat of Chennai could be oppressive. I took my laptop to check emails and messages. Oh! Those days before smartphones! Or at least before I got one. As I was scrolling through my mails, I saw one from someone I knew very well. I opened it. It was oozing with sugary words and expressions of love and affection. I felt bile rising in my throat. She was in the US and I had made several attempts to see her and every time she was elusive. And now she was crying about how much she wanted to see me. I ignored it. I did not respond. I had over a period of time learned to ignore and weed out fake people from my life. I was all the better for that.

Although secretly many talked to me, their spouses or family didn't want me around. What's with women who think that a single woman is but there to steal their men??? How insecure are they about their marriage and themselves too??? My thoughts meandered through myriads of experiences in no particular order. But it always brought me to a place of peace and left me with a smile on my lips. I may have dozed off at some point.

My daughter-in-law was slowly tapping me on my shoulders. She asked me to go and lie down. I agreed and went in.

CHAPTER 8

It was two days later that she got back to me on the same balcony, over the morning coffee. She started the conversation as though there had been no break.

She: So how long did you stay with that lady?

Me: A couple of months. After a week, she could see that I was getting restless. I had nothing to do. Those days, even looking for a job while on a visitor's visa was an offence. But I thought it would be well worth it to do a job search. I could at least get an idea of the job market. So thus began my new quest. Most jobs required certification and a valid visa making me eligible to work in the US and I didn't have either. I was a tourist.

I still dared to go ahead and apply. My intention was only to see what the market was like. I had no confidence in myself as I was repeatedly reminded when I was still a student, back home, that I had done my education on a whim. No plans, no focus. A drifter. That may have been right. But it never went wrong for me. On the contrary, it all worked out for me.

I paused for a moment to rewind in my head and

reminisce that part of my life, where I was validated as a very competent person. I took a deep breath and sighed – a sigh of accomplishment and contentment.

Her voice cut into my thoughts, "How did you end up with a circus? I know you sent us pictures on and off … but why the circus ma? You could have taught in any school in the US". I looked into her eyes and thought to myself, "This is the mildest form of inquisition I will be facing, just a beginning to the life I am now going to face".

I chose my words carefully as I began narrating the story.

"Simple. I dared", I told her.

Dared to take chances.

Dared to be different.

Dared to trust my Creator.

So basically detachment, distancing, dispassion seemed to be the way to go if I had to survive.

Let me go back a little bit, to the first job and how it all marked the start of my learning while teaching. The first one started with a feeling of total accomplishment. Here I was in a strange cold country with nothing familiar except some Hollywood movies to fall back on. I felt empowered that I came alone and I was able to find a job, with a valid visa. All this at a time when no one was being granted visas, at a time the country was very strictly monitoring those who came in on a tourist visa but were trying to get employed. I did not ever do anything dishonest or illegal. I simply dared. I was willing to take a leap. Unless I leaped, I wouldn't know, would I? It paid off. There was a lot of paperwork which had to be set in motion before the approval came. All I would have before me would be an email from an attorney who was working on my visa. I haven't studied law or immigration. Therefore, going back to the attorney and asking the meaning of the jargon used in the legal world was probably my first education. Step by step, I stayed on track, followed the lead and gathered all the papers (read certificates) I could. Once again, I was feeling amazed at how "a bunch of useless papers" to my own people back home turned out to be the very same things that were fetching me the job in the US of A. However, not without verification and accreditation. Fully legit. Therefore, the first set of loops for me were the evaluation of my certificates. Here I was sitting before an interview board who had no questions about my credentials or experience. All they wanted to know was would I be able to speak in a way they could understand, and if I would be able to understand their accent; in a nutshell, would I be able to cope with their American English. I passed the test in less than 10 minutes. By the time, the panel of about half a dozen people had questioned me. I was offered the job and asked to get on with the paper work.

For my first day at work in the land of opportunities as it is called, the US of A, I walked in with a lot of confidence. Special Ed was my passion. I loved taking what seems daunting and making it work. I walked into the room of the head of the school with my usual greeting. She looked up and looked at me as though a worm had crawled into her room. This was not what I had expected. My heart sank. Was she having a bad day? Or had I said something wrong to her during the interview, or perhaps she had never liked me. "Could you please wait outside for a few minutes?" she said with a smile that never reached her eyes. I nodded and stepped out. I waited a full 30 minutes at least before she came out and told me to go to the class as it was time for the students to come in. I had not been told which class or what age group. Seeing the look on my face, she said a tad impatiently, "Here, let me walk you down to your class". I did not miss that note of impatience in her voice. I was led into a class of teenagers, both boys and girls. They were loud and boisterous. They sort of quietened down when they saw the head of the school. They spared me a glance and listened to her introduce me. As soon as she said I was their homeroom teacher, there was a loud guffaw and they looked at me with the "And-the-Fun-Begins" look. The head of the school barely spared me a look. As she walked out of the room, she said over her shoulders, "Call me if you need something". I just knew instinctively she would never pick my call.

Here I was standing in a lion's den. I took a deep breath and said, "Good Morning. Let me first introduce myself".

One boy, clearly the one that leads the pack, said, "It doesn't matter to us who you are". I was taken aback but continued nevertheless. My name is … you can call me Ms. Manna. All kinds of comments were being passed but I was determined to finish my prepared introductory talk. I felt my mouth go dry, I felt like everything was becoming blurry. I turned to the board to hide my tears. I wrote my name on the board, said a prayer and turned around, and with a smile that hurt my face said, "Now, let me hear about you". One boy said, "My mother was killed". I just nodded. All laughed. I did not know what to say. I said softly, "I'm sorry to hear that" – I had learned that from the movies. But I don't remember seeing people laugh at the death of someone's mother. I was on unchartered waters.

Me: And what is your name?

He: Why do you want my name? Are you going to do a check on me?

Me: I don't need to check on anyone. I will trust what I see with my own eyes.

Finally, I spoke with conviction. Truth has a way of standing up for itself, doesn't it? This was the best thing I could have said and it came out of nowhere. I knew that by the expression on the faces of the students, I seemed to have touched a chord. But the pack leader was not going to give in easily. He said with a sneer, "His mother was not killed. She is alive and she has been called in to school today". More laughter. By now I didn't know what to believe and what not to believe. Then before I got a chance to say anything, the boy who claimed his mother was killed exploded. He jumped up and kicked the boy who called his bluff and the next thing I knew chairs were flying out the window. Everyone was fighting with everyone, girls kicking boys and a volley of cuss words. I stood rooted, paralyzed – behaviour disorder and emotional disturbance at its peak. I just moved into the middle of all this scuffle, a puny 5'4" in the midst of all these almost 6 footers. It was as if they were putting up a mock situation for me to handle – testing waters, pushing my button. Suddenly everyone just moved back and all of a sudden, they all turned against me. "Did you just touch me?" yelled one girl. She was the queen bee of the class. Maybe that was unexpected and inappropriate – inappropriate because you never touch a student ever without permission! Another lesson learned the hard way. As I stood there in utter shock and confusion, she said, "Don't touch me, Bitch!" I have no idea where I got the strength from. I said as loudly as I could, "Sit down, NOW". All of a sudden, they all sat. By now, as if on cue, the head turned up at the door.

"What's going on here?" she demanded. The whole class started talking together, each sounding louder than the other. She turned to me and, in front of the students and in a tone that was humiliating, repeated the question,

"What's going on here?" My tongue was sticking to the roof of my mouth. My stomach churned and just as I opened my mouth to say something, one of the girls spoke, "It is not her fault. She didn't have a chance with Edmond and Patrick here". I could have hugged her. The rest remained silent. The head of the school turned and as she left once again said, "Would like you to sit in for the parent meeting with Patrick's mother?" The mother who was supposedly killed was going to be sitting in front of me. The rest of the day had highs and lows. But it went by until 2.30 pm. The class dismissed. After the students left, I looked around and saw how dirty it was – wrappers of chocolates, food crumbs, cartons of juice bottles everywhere. I sat on my chair, tired. Beaten. The strength or courage that I thought I had was nowhere to be seen or felt. I was not going to make it. Then, all of a sudden, I remembered that I had to meet the mother-who-was-killed at 3 pm. I went to the rest room, washed my face. I met another teacher there and she blanked me out too. We Indians can be completely invisible or totally repulsive. I do not want to generalize but it happens on and off. Just that, on that day, it was on.

I walked to the meeting room with a notepad to make notes. But as soon as I reached there, the head asked, "Where is Patrick's file?"

"I don't know", I replied.

"You don't know? You are the homeroom teacher

and you have to know who the students are. It should be in the cabinet in your class". I walked back in humiliation to the classroom and opened the cabinet. There were a million files. Which one am I supposed to pick? Finally, I picked the first one with "Patrick" on it. I walked back to the meeting room and there was Patrick, the mother-who-was-killed, and the head. It clearly was a no-win situation. I sat down. The mother was too preoccupied to even notice me. I was introduced as Patrick's homeroom teacher. The intonation implied that I was going to be responsible for all things bad. It did not matter that it was my first working day. So, the meeting started with the head starting a long list of things Patrick was not doing (which he was supposed to do) and how that would impact his court hearing. I almost fell off the chair. What had I let myself into??? The biblical Daniel-in-the-lion's-den seemed like a piece of cake. The mother sat there helplessly. If there is one thing parenting has taught me, it is to never make any parent feel bad at a parent-teacher meeting. They are all trying their best. My innate empathy kicked in. I reached out and touched the mother's arm, looked into her eyes and said, "There is always a solution for everything. Going by the first day in class, I think Patrick and I can work something out. Won't we Patrick?" I cannot explain the look that appeared on the mother's face. Relief? Gratitude? Helplessness? Suddenly I knew I had made a break through this insurmountable wall.

Patrick immediately as meek as a lamb said, "Yes. I am sorry that …" I did not allow him to complete the sentence. I said, "Everything that's happened until this moment is behind us. We start afresh tomorrow. What do you say?" He gave me a fist pump. The first fist pump of my life (Also, from the Hollywood movies). The meeting ended victoriously for me. My heart was singing. My body was tired. My mind was lifted in gratitude to the Almighty, who always and always looks out for me. Kindness wins always.

This is not life on celluloid, where, from the next day, everything just fell into place. This was my real life. And that meant, there were many more fist-fights, many more name calling events and many more meetings. Not all parents were easy to handle. Some came in drunk, some high on drugs, some angry and so looking for a punching bag. Three-and-a-half months of this and I threw in the towel. The trigger was during one of the fist-fights in which a boy got punched in his face, and he started bleeding from his nose. I grabbed the tissue box, made a wad and held it and left the class towards the office. When I reached there, out came the head and her first words, "You DO NOT ever leave the class unattended". I longed to be omnipresent. I handed Michael over to her and went back to the class after washing my hands. There was a lot of laughter and giggling. One kid said, "You better wash your hands well … he is HIV+". I somehow saw the day through. As I walked out at the end of the day, I stopped by the office to see if I could meet someone. There was one of the teachers whom I had seen during staff meetings. He was the only one who was kind. He had once told me, "Don't give up, you will soon get the hang of it". On that day, I wanted to just hug him and cry. But I didn't. Instead, I told him what had happened in class. He was guarded when he answered but he said, "They should have shared the medical details of the students with you". I didn't want to hear anything more. My mind was made up. I wanted to go back home. It was a Wednesday. I went back to school on Thursday and went to the office and asked for the medical file of the students. I was told I will be given those before the end of the day. It never came to me. On Friday, I went back with my resignation letter. At the end of the day, I handed the letter and walked away. I did not hesitate to say that I did not fit in there. For the first time, I saw the head smile. She wanted to hug me and say her "goodbye". Bitch! I could never say that aloud. We didn't use those words back home where I came from. But that evening when I looked into the mirror before my bath, I said it out aloud ... BITCH! It is always tough when you use it for the first time. Then it comes naturally. To the world, the job in the Nation's capital seemed like the best thing. And in a way, indeed, it was the best thing. But the culture shock was too much. The students were wild – huge strapping young men and women really, with both emotional and behavioural disorder. I couldn't cope. I felt after just 3 months in a new country, this was far out of bounds for me. My thought one evening as I sipped my hot chocolate with whipped cream from my favourite coffee shop was, "Why come all the way across the oceans to be either shot or stabbed to death, when my own people would have eventually done that for me subtly, slowly, but surely!" So, I quit … Without a second thought, without looking at the consequences. I had a 3-year H1B visa. What I didn't know was, the visa would be cancelled by the employer if and when I quit. It was only when I talked to my attorney that I realized that I would in the next 3 months become an illegal immigrant if I didn't find another job. So, my attorney who was by now annoyed with me told me to go back to the Board of Directors and ask them to hold on until I found another job. This I did.

The Director of the management called me to find out why I left. I said, "I'm going back home. I miss my children". He was a very kind man. He was the one who had actually hired me. He said, "I'm sorry you are leaving us, but I understand". That was how my first hope at starting out fresh in a new country panned out for me.

I slept through the weekend. I didn't tell my children that I had quit. I didn't tell anyone. I stayed indoors all of Saturday and Sunday thinking what next!

Many thoughts came through my mind. One end of the spectrum was, "Take the first flight home". The other end was to go back and beg for the job. On Saturday, the thought of going home won. By the time it was Monday morning, I felt strong enough to find a new job. But it was a good 3 to 4 months before I got my second job. By then I had exhausted whatever little money I had. I couldn't afford the rental place. That's when a friend mentioned to me about a students' hostel in the same town that I was. The hostel was called India House. Another sign?

CHAPTER 9

India House was a youth hostel which was a place a lot like a rundown lodge in India. It had rooms which were overflowing with youngsters. All rooms were dormitory style and get this … mixed dorms. I walked into that place, where nothing appealed to me, only because I needed shelter. They charged $16 a day. I could barely manage that. On looking back, I see that it was a blessing. It cured me of my snobbishness; it smoothened my judgmental airs to a certain extent; it taught me to appreciate the small things. This was again Christmas time, and in contrast to the previous year, here I was sitting with no glitter, no lights, no Christmas dinner and no money for a full square meal. How soon life changes for some!

The place carried a musty smell, like that of a closed damp room. There were oil heaters in every room, which hardly worked. I kept getting calls from home from children and friends asking about my Christmas plans. I had none. I lied and concocted plans. There was a severe snowstorm one evening and all of us were snowed in.

There was a convenience store right across the hostel. It was run by Jamaicans and they kept it open. They sold something similar to our puffs. It was so close in taste to our Indian puffs. I would walk across and get one every now and then. That would be my food for an entire day. It was the same that day, and as all of us huddled into the lounge area, I met this young lady from Dominican Republic who now lived in Florida. We got talking. She was a social worker and was there to spend Christmas with her friends. But the snowstorms across the east coast messed up the plans and she was stranded there.

She was a kind person. She decided we were going to celebrate Christmas one way or the other. She walked across to the store, bought two slices of chocolate cakes and a bottle of wine. We opened it in our room that night, greeted each other for Christmas and exchanged more stories of each other's culture. She remained my friend for a long time. Another random act of kindness made my Christmas bearable. At least I didn't have to spend it alone in the room, cold, miserable and sad.

The next day, the owner of the place came by and ordered a huge turkey and some drinks for those stranded there. That was a nice gesture. It was free Christmas dinner, on the house. So, after all, in a run-down hostel, named after my home country, with no lights and glitter, with no family or friends, I had a good Christmas, with glistening snow, new friends and strangers acting like family.

This hostel had a rule. Guests were not allowed to stay for more than 2 weeks. I ended up being there for almost 2 months. The owner just looked the other way and the caretaker, I assume, just protected me. I have no explanations to how and why these things happened. However, I always felt an inner peace that I knew was not earthly.

CHAPTER 10

The next couple of months were distressing. Money ran out. Friends were becoming few and far between, and my meals had dwindled to once a day. But I was not going to give up. I kept looking for jobs whenever I could access a computer. That's when the opportunity came from Chicago. I grabbed on to it as a drowning man to the straw. This sounded safer. I could stay on the campus of the school inclusive of food. The pay was almost half of what I was earning in my first job. But then accommodation, food and expense to commute added up to more than what I was getting from my first job. When I went for the interview, there were two conditions. First, if I wanted to live in their quarters, I would have to do the job of a dorm parent. Second, I would have to learn driving and have a driver's licence by the end of 3 months or I would lose the job. I agreed right away. I had no plan as to how I would get a licence or learn driving. But at that moment, I needed the job. My thinking was that at least for 3 months I would have a safe place to stay and food to eat. I hardly knew anyone in Chicago. Then an old friend of mine introduced me to his partner Paul, who lived there. We became friends. He was an angel sent from above. He volunteered to teach me driving with his car, his gas and his time. Thus, in 3 months, I owned a license. Most evenings were spent driving around the neighbourhood of the school. The roads in the suburbs were easy to manoeuvre. It gave me enough time to master the steering balance. There were no lanes to stay in. No traffic lights to stop, pause or move. We just drove around and may be passed a car or two in an hour. It worked well to build up my confidence. Then, Paul took me to the town roads. Here the roads had two lanes only. So that was fine too. I had to now learn to watch for road signs and traffic lights. It was easy. I could do a smooth stop and a smooth start. Driving on these roads always ended up pulling into a burger place where we practised parking. Reversing into a parking spot and pulling out of one were driving skills I had to learn. It was a piece of cake. Paul was one of the best driving instructors in the whole world. His patience, dedication and commitment, especially considering it was at no cost, were commendable. We usually ended up manoeuvring the drive through and ordering a burger. It is rare to find a friend like that. In a month's time, he managed to get me on to the expressway, and I was able to drive, maintaining the speed limit expected. I had become a steady, smooth driver on the road. My driving was better than my life thus far. Within a month, I was a proud owner of the Illinois driver's licence.

Talking about the driver's licence was easy and a pleasant memory. However, going for the actual driver's test was not so pleasant. I failed the first test. I am not someone who is normally over-sensitive to discriminations. However, my first test was one which I had to do under a clearly hostile environment. From the moment that the lady from the Department of Motor Vehicles took her place beside me, she was emitting a vibe which made me uncomfortable.

She: "How long have you been on the road?" (sceptical)

Me: "A month" (Nervously)

She: "A month? And you think you are ready for the roads in US!" (sneer)

She continues: "People come from all over the world, sit behind a wheel for a month and they think they are ready for the licence. This country has rules and regulations unlike most other countries". (Rant)

I bit my tongue. I wanted to get out of the car on some street in Lake Forest, Illinois, and walk all the way back home to India. I failed my test. I am pretty brave when it comes to taking failures, but not when it is unfairly thrust upon me. So, what do you think I did? I went back for the test the very next day. This time I took a convertible which was owned by a friend at church. I have no clue what I would have done if the same lady had been the one testing me. However, when you go forward with no fear and with a determination to conquer defeat, things just fall into place. I had a visibly pregnant lady get into the seat beside me. She smiled at me and in the gentlest voice told me to relax and take the car. I felt a flood of gratitude sweep over me. Even if I failed, it would be a gentle respectful one. However, the plans were different for me that day. She asked me to take a road which was one straight road. She asked me why I was in the US and if I had my family with me. I explained why I was alone and so far away from "home". She then told me how she was dumped as soon as the man realized she was pregnant. My heart went out to her. We drove around a bit longer in style in a convertible talking like we were best of friends. God knew that we both needed each other. She needed me as much as I needed my licence. I went back with my licence and job security.

I could now continue there for the next 2 years. Once the job was secured, I began to focus on that and realized that it was just a job. No challenges, the easiest piece of work I had ever done. People were not discriminatory. The school itself had Asian students in residence. So even if there were some patronizing remarks on and off, it was nothing compared to what drove me away from my own land in the first place, or made me run away from my first job. There was no threat to my life.

So, I sucked it up. There is no perfect world, a lesson I was beginning to learn rather fast. There were only perfect attitudes.

When you are in a place of routine, or inertia, you become that. I don't mean to say that there was no activity in a school full of high-school students. But when you have students who are totally focused and on task all the time, there is nothing left for the teacher to do. I cannot believe I am saying this, but I have now swung to a diametrically opposite side, from my previous job. Girls were polite, intelligent, near-perfection. That didn't work for me. After my traumatic experience in DC, here I was 3 months later talking of "nothing happening". Doing study-time supervision was pure boredom. What kind of teens were these, not wanting to do anything amiss! My heart, mind and soul longed for action and adventure. I would go to the public library on my day off to use their computers. I didn't want to job search from the school computers for obvious reasons. Nothing seemed to be of any particular interest. My choices were as wide as the country itself. I had no particular interest to be employed in any one State. I did this for several days and it was on one such day when I had almost given up finding a new job, that my eyes fell upon the words "Travelling Teacher". I was intrigued. Little did I know that it was the beginning of an adventure of a life time. Never did I realize that I was going to be walking through a door and would be entering into the Heart of the Circus. And thus would begin the Chronicles of Manna.

My daughter-in-law sat enthralled by this narration. I would look at her occasionally and see disbelief flit in and through her eyes. She changed gears. "But how did you end up with a circus?" I smiled and said, "That's a story for another day. It's a long story. Let's get our breakfast".

CHAPTER 11

At breakfast I was quiet and thoughtful. Breaking the silence I said, "I have to tell you about my adventures at the Chicago school before I tell you about my circus life". Suddenly I broke out into a big smile and continued, "The best part of my life up to this point was I got an H1B visa after entering with a visit visa in a short span of time … another miracle and a sign to go forward. I rested to recoup from the trauma of that first job and found my second job.

But I dared to … I always loved to take up a dare. Except I had no idea how I was going to learn driving. But then Paul steps in. The reason for the licence was while taking up the duty of a dorm parent meant I had free board and food, it also meant that I would have to drive the resident students around the town to get grocery, or to and from the airport for their travel. Also, there were planned cultural activities over weekends like trying out ethnic food, or visiting different places of worship. Thus, my driving was upgraded from a regular car to a mini school bus. This experience helped me understand why folks in big vehicles would easily turn bullies on the road. But driving on the highway in heavy traffic, parking at the airport, a small thing like getting the parking token from the dispensing machine while leaning over with my foot still on the brakes were too much for me. I would stop the vehicle completely and then get the parking token. By then the impatient drivers behind me would be freaking out. Oh! The ordeal!!! My job was a piece of cake. But now, here I was driving a mini school bus about 25 miles to the airport and back a couple of times in a year. That's when I thought, maybe, I should look for something more interesting. There wasn't much to keep myself active or my life interesting. Be careful when you send a thought into the Universe, it will come right back at you as a wish granted. The driving around (read as risk taking) was the only thing that excited me about the job. Otherwise, it was a totally unchallenging job, which got me bored very fast. My first real drive was to the airport to pick up students coming back from their winter breaks. I had had lessons in driving, but not driving in a snow storm.

That unforgettable day, I wore a pair of jeans, a t-shirt, a sweater and my usual sandals and headed out to the airport. It was a crisp cold morning. It was cloudy, but I figured I could return before it started raining. I reached the airport on time, parked without any mishap and entered the arrival area to wait for the students. They were arriving on two separate flights – six from Korea and two from Japan. The Korean girls arrived and as usual they greeted me with controlled emotions and a wisp of a smile. Their eyes did show love and joy through those tiny slits. I had learned to understand them. They chattered away in their language among themselves. I waited for the arrival of the other two which was only less than an hour later. After collecting them, as I walked out to get the vehicle, I stood in shock. It had begun to snow. Now how do I drive? The wind chill was already piercing through me. I had to get the vehicle from the parking lot to the pick-up point, as these girls had a lot of luggage. I walked towards the vehicle. The girls were thankfully unaware of my predicament. Do I switch-on the wiper? Do I go at normal speed? Slow? Fast? All the pictures of vehicles skidding off the road (thank you movies!) kept playing on my mind. Somehow carefully, slowly, I pulled the vehicle out and brought it to the pick-up point. The girls loaded their luggage and got in. My feet (in sandals, mind you) were beginning to go numb.

One of the girls politely reminded me to turn on the heat in the bus. I didn't know how to! I had learned driving in summer, so had not thought of turning on the heat. And what would I know about the same switch that turned the AC on would also work for the heat! One of the Korean girls, who had some knowledge about driving and some common sense, got up and came forward and turned on the heat. This now fogged up the mirror and now what do I do? Turn the wiper on. How do I do that??? The same girl came forward as I was driving and showed me. By now the snow was falling like someone was playing a nasty prank on me. Sensing my anxiety, the girls stopped chattering and paid attention to my driving, encouraging me and asking me to drive as slow as I wanted. "No one pulls you up for driving slow during bad weather", said a soft voice from behind me. My glasses were fogging up or was it due to the tears welling up in my eyes? After 25 miles of excruciating driving through the thick snowfall and the highway, I managed to reach the school without a scratch on anyone. The Resident Head was waiting anxiously for us. She looked at my exposed toes as I parked my vehicle and walked towards her. "Shoes and socks from now on Manna", she said firmly. That was the extent of my excitement at this job. I soon got bored. I could feel the restlessness build up inside me. Lots of free time and the working hours barely posed any challenge. I became a pro at driving both Paul's car and the school van. Now what?

My weekends used to be spent with a family who were then in Chicago. If anything, that was my excitement during my 2 years in Chicago. We have had such fun trips to malls, restaurants and Indian stores. They were relatives by marriage. It is strange how much fun I have had with them. Lots and lots of laughter and fun things.

One time the nephew had gone on a visit to India and I was there with his wife and two kids. He had said we could use his car. We sure did use it!!!! It was all great until one day we had an accident and lost one of the side mirrors. We were in a panic. The nephew would return in two days and he would be mad. We didn't have a clue where to look for car parts. Like I said before, I can sit behind a steering wheel and drive. Nothing else. I sent an SOS to Paul, my friend. As usual he was there with a solution. He said we might find the exact same model in a junkyard where they sold spare parts. Therefore, we headed off to a junkyard. Long story short, we managed to have it fixed – except that the mirror on the left was very different from the mirror on the right!!! Like ostriches, we believed since he would be driving on the left, he may never see the one on the right. WRONG! It was the first thing he noticed when we went to pick him up at the airport. Busted!

CHAPTER 12

After breakfast, everyone started going their separate ways. They had to get to work, or finish off chores, run errands or take the kids to school. By 9 am I was left alone at home with their dog. She was very content resting by my feet. She would sense my mood through the calls I would make through the day. I was grateful to her because she was so unconditionally loving. I had picked up my Kindle to read. *The Secret Life of Bees*. Soothing and easy to read. By the end of it, I realized it was about Forgiveness.

"Yes", I told myself. That is where I must begin. My rebirth on Indian soil. By forgiving without compromising on my being. I also knew that I had to start with myself. Even in my thoughts I got defensive. What's the need for me to forgive? I didn't think I could do anything wrong. I believed or my ego allowed me to believe that I was infallible. My biggest struggle was finding what I needed to set right. I always thought that I could never go wrong, you see.

I had the house to myself, the thoughts to myself

and absolutely no distractions. I sat by the window watching life pass by. I saw a mom start her two-wheeler and a little girl in a school uniform climbing on to the pillion and holding the mom tight around her waist. The revving Scooty spewed the impatience of the mother. In a second, they were gone. Then I saw a street vendor push a cart of vegetables, and as he called out loudly, his wares and their prices, many stay-at-home moms came out and were soon buying vegetables and exchanging pleasantries. I looked at the clock it was 9.10 am and I knew the next day I would see the exact same scene if I looked out the window. The working mom taking her kid to school, the street vendor, the stay-at-home moms buying the vegetables. I also knew that this would be repeated day after day. If I looked through the window the next day and the next and the next, the same scene would be repeated. Then I realized how the landscape had changed a million times as I looked out of my window the last two decades. The thoughts sent me back to the private school in Chicago, where I had a good view out of my window. It gave me a view of the changing seasons, the changing colours of the leaves, the snow-laden trees, and then the fresh new leaves and flowers, the coloured leaves to bare boughs. How life had gathered speed when I moved from the serene life to a chaotic one on a circus! How the view outside my window would change every second!

My daughter-in-law got back earlier than usual, grabbed a glass of water and came and sat by me. "It was difficult to focus at work. Also, I was wondering if you were OK on your own", she said smiling. I knew she wanted to hear it all. I smiled at her naïve curiosity. Do I tell her *everything*? Or do I go with what she asks only? She cuts no slack. She picks up where she left off. "So, how did you land with the circus?"

I made myself comfortable on the sofa and started: It was 2004, about a year and a half into my Chicago life. I had driven a mini bus, I had driven through snow, walked with flip flops in the snow. But nothing seemed to be exciting enough for me. I was bored. I wanted more challenges. So, I started browsing through the job portals and found a vacancy for a "Travelling Teacher". I applied out of sheer curiosity. As always, a million questions came rushing in.

How would I travel? Whom would I teach? Where would I travel? Within Florida? Or the East coast? Or? ... I needed to know. I sat before my computer and filled out an application and hit "send". In less than 15 minutes, I got a call.

The lady, after the initial pleasantries, said, "Your application stood out among the thousands". I raised my eyebrows in total shock. Was she being sarcastic? Remember how I was always told I was unfocussed and had no goal. All the people who had always scorned me on my unplanned education flashed through my mind. Mathematics to Literature to Special Ed to Pastoral Counselling to General Counselling ... like a monkey jumping from one branch to another, purposeless but loving it. Somewhere in between was a diploma in IATA too! Anyway, through all these thoughts, the voice at the other end cut in: "We would like to fly you to Detroit for an interview ASAP".

Again, my usual style, with no thought of caution, no stopping to think, no fear of the unknown, I gave this stranger my personal details and hoped I would get my tickets and not have my bank looted. I waited for the tickets that would take me to the place which would solve the mystery of the travelling teacher. I was not committed as yet, I told myself. I still had the choice of saying "NO" if I found the job impossible to handle or risky. But I was determined to know what this "Travelling Teacher" was expected to do. No stretch of imagination was getting me a satisfactory answer.

The same evening, I had my tickets in hand to head out to Detroit. I took a couple of days off from work, and headed out to Detroit. They put me in the suite of a nice hotel. And I was thinking: "The life of a travelling teacher begins!! I could get used to this". I looked around the impressive room and the large bathroom with a bath tub. I decided to soak myself in the bath. I ran the water and slid into its warmth. It felt good. I ordered some dinner and settled down to watch some TV. I picked up my digital camera (those were the days of digital cameras) and tried to capture what I thought was my new home. A suite with room service, which might end up being my new lifestyle! I sent the pictures by email to my sons. I impressed them. Then I went to bed early, as I knew I had a big day coming up.

The next day, I was picked up and taken to the location of my interview. It was an Arena. (Remember even at this point I had no clue it was going to be a circus!)

My conversation with the guy who picked me up, after the greetings and stuff:

Me: So where is the office?

He: What office?

Me: The office of the manager.

He: Oh! He's at the Arena.

Me: Silence ... Arena? (I didn't voice it)

Soon in about 10 minutes, we were pulling into a place with huge cut-outs of clowns, dancing girls and there were even cut-outs of a few elephants and tigers.

He stopped the car, got out and started walking. I followed him and was soon engulfed by blaring music and live clowns whisked past me on skate boards. I was sick. For the first time, I was shaken. I'm so scared of clowns (thank you Enid Blyton!). I was led back stage. And there behind the curtains sat a portly bald man on a black box (which later I would learn was used to pack circus props).

I hug my file close to myself tightly and say "Good Morning, Sir".

He: Sir? There are no sirs here. (He said with a grin). You can call me Jack.

I nod. I'm more aware of clowns running around me.

His voice cuts through my fear, "So, Ms. Manna, are you ready for the circus???" My mouth went dry.

My tongue stuck to the roof of my mouth. Circus? Me? I'm not at all athletic, I hate moving my body except when absolutely necessary. What can I teach at the circus?

My wits as usual came to my rescue. I smiled, pulled myself up, and said, "Almost ... But I have questions".

He: Of course! Shoot!

Me: Who are my students?

I held my breath. I needed the job.

He: We have performers from all over the world. Their children need to be in school. Also those performers who are under the age of 18 must attend school. You will teach them. All subjects and all grades.

Phew! I just needed to exercise my brain not my body. Although I didn't understand it all, I was partly relieved.

Me: How many students are there? "From all over the world" kept reverberating in my ears.

He: Right now, four.

"That's easy!" I thought.

He: Come, let me take you to the class. You can meet the teacher and the students.

So, we walked through the costumed human figures and loud music, and entered a room. My first set of students! They turned away with unhappy faces when I was introduced. Their teacher of several years was leaving to get married. And this strange coloured lady was replacing her. I guess they thought there were too many adjustments to be made. After introducing me to the teacher and suggesting I may be her replacement, Mr. Jack went away.

I was left there to learn the ropes. The more I stayed in the classroom, the more I realized there were no ropes. I knew I had my work cut out for me.

I tried making conversations with the students. It didn't work.

I tried asking the teacher for the curriculum. There wasn't any.

I tried asking, "In which hotel do you stay?" She replied, "Oh! I have a room on the train".

What a strange answer! She didn't think my question whether she lived in a hotel strange either. (I would later learn that some folks didn't live on the train but rode in company vehicles to the next town and lived in hotels). More and more ambiguity was all I was getting by spending the day with the teacher.

A couple of hours later, I left, heavy hearted, because all the places that I had worked until then, I was loved by the students. Here they hated me.

I went back to the manager and he asked me what I thought.

I said, faking confidence, "Oh! I'm excited". I needed the job very badly.

"But Mr. Jack, what about my stay?"

He: Ah! Your stay. Follow Mr. Jack (He laughs. Was there a tinge of sarcasm?)

Later I would learn there were no "sirs" or "Mr." tags to anyone's names. All were addressed by first names. All my convent primary education for nothing!!!

I digress ...

I followed Mr. Jack to the car park. He pulled out a white truck and asked me to hop in. Soon I was in a white truck, with a stranger, heading to an unknown destination.

I was lost in my memories but a sharp intake of breath brought me down to Earth. It was my daughter-in-law. She looked at me with a look of both disbelief and "are-you-stupid". I smiled reading her thoughts and continued, "Yes I know, it was stupid".

"No no, not stupid", she began and then said, "Well, maybe, a little stupid ..." We laughed together and she urged me to continue.

I continued, "A few curves and turns and lonely dirt roads later I found myself bumping over railway tracks. By now I was convinced I was in trouble and there was nothing I could do. Here I was in a strange country, with a strange man, in a white pick-up truck, driving through strange terrain. Tears welled up in my eyes. I kept my head turned away, looking out of the window. Is this how my life was going to end? My imagination ran amok. He didn't notice my consternation or my tears. Suddenly he broke into my thoughts.

He: Look that's your new home. (Pointing to a shiny silver train!)

And yes! We were riding by a silvery train shimmering in the sun which had the logo "The Greatest Show". He stopped by a coach and climbed on it. He turned around and asked me to follow him. It smelled of fresh paint. It was spotlessly clean.

He: (opening a door) This is your home.

I didn't then know that this tiny 7 × 12 space would be my home for the next few years.

Here's what I saw inside:

On my left, there was a small table with seats on either side which converted to a bed if need be – more like a booth at a restaurant. Above that was a bed, a bunk bed. On the right was a sink, a stove, a fridge, a microwave and ample cabinets for storage. Behind me was a door which opened into a tiny shower and the toilet. Before entering the toilet, on my right was a full-length mirror which was on a door. When I opened it, I realized that it was a closet for clothes.

"You are lucky. This is a new coach so it's spotlessly clean", his voice cut into my thoughts. We got off the train.

He offered to drive me back to the hotel. My flight was the next morning. So, I got to enjoy the suite one more night. As he dropped me off at the hotel, he said, "We will fly you to Tampa, Florida, in a week's time".

"Thank you, Mr. Jack".

He smiled, shook his head, at my "Mr." Jack.

The truck drove off as I whispered to the chill air around me, "Was that a job offer?"

I live in the moment most of the time. And so I told myself, "To the warm bath first …"

You see, some people go to the US of A and become the VP of the country. I just went and became an on-location-educator! "Sounds grander than a circus teacher, doesn't it?" I asked with a smile. I continued, "That designation is what I used when talking to all of you. I didn't want to shock family and friends by labelling myself as a 'circus girl'. At that moment, I had no time to waste thinking of labels and opinions. I needed that job. My older son was already in college in the US and I needed to support as much as I could. What anyone thought or what it would do to the reputation of the family did not matter at that point".

Mr. Jack kept his word; a week later I found myself in Tampa, Florida. As usual, I travelled light.

My clothes and toiletries were packed into a suitcase, along with a few CDs (my feel-good songs) and my daily devotional book and a few of my favourite books.

My resilience, my desire to explore, my belligerence with spurts of kindness and compassion all made me a complex being. Standing tall and strong when the familiar world around one is shaken, bouncing back in no time, the innate knowledge that all are equal were thoughts alien to the world I had come from. I could not handle and was always close to asphyxiation. I could just allow that, or I could break free from it all. The choice was mine. [My conversations at different times with my children were cathartic. They always helped clearing my mind and helped me gain a perspective of me and my life.]

CHAPTER 13

Tampa, Florida, was beautiful. I stepped off the plane and found it a lot warmer than Chicago, more like our own Kerala. I was here for the first time. I knew nothing about Florida except for a few titbits of conversations from movies. As I rolled my suitcase out of the airport, doubts, fear and near-panic hit me. All I had was an address. Standing on the curb-side, where I was completely oblivious of the sign that said it was the spot for cab pickup, I asked a passer-by, "Where can I get a cab?" He looked at the sign and then at me, probably considering if I was visually impaired. He silently pointed to the sign almost above my head, smiled and walked on. We are not used to signs. We Indians love to do just that – stand right under a sign and ask someone for directions! I felt like an imbecile. I hailed a cab and told myself, "Be alert! Enough folly for the day!" I gave the cheery cab driver the address. I was so afraid that he would hear my heart pounding. Then suddenly I thought of the many women back in India, my family, friends, and all the other renowned women. Not one of them would do this. Not because they were not brave or bold, but because they would pause to think. I am not sure if I am impulsive or just bold. I left them all behind in the past and focused on the here and now. The driver took me through some places which showed houses with plantain trees, jackfruit tree, papaya and curry leaves. I smiled and felt happy being in familiar surroundings. I could have been in my little state back in India. That bliss was short-lived. The driver made a sharp turn to the right and I found myself being driven through an unpaved road, grease on the ground, and a lot of train tracks. My instinct was to turn around and go to the main road. Back home, that would have been just the kind of an area where women were forbidden from being seen. But I had to keep going. I remembered the ride with Mr. Jack over the bumpy tracks. It was like deja vu. The feeling of having been there before, yet not familiar with anything. Reality! I'm going to my new home on the train. I felt nervous. I was going to make my home among strangers, in a strange place, in an even stranger home. I had a suitcase ... that's it! My belongings, if that's what you would call a few books and my music (CDs), had to be left behind in Chicago with my only friend Paul.

All of a sudden, I felt tears in my eyes ... I knew no one here, no friends, no family ... I wanted to see my sons. I wanted to go back to what I knew all my life. I'd rather be browbeaten by family and friends than face this highwire act. This probably is why women stay in oppressive situations, I thought to myself. A known devil is better than an unknown. I took a deep breath and said this, even as I declined the invitation to the pity party, "I'm going to meet the unknown devil and I'm going to dance with it". The driver stopped the cab. I paid him and stood there in front of the glistening silver snake. I read the logo "The Greatest Show". "Indeed!" I told myself. It was going to be the Greatest Show on Earth that I was going to put up. That's when I saw a petite lady walking towards me with a warm smile. She held out her hand even as she asked,

"*Manna?*"

I said, "Yes". (Someone knew my name!!)

She: You must be tired. Let's go find your room.

I followed her and soon found myself in the same room that was shown to me during my interview in Detroit.

The lady, Bea, started giving me a "tour" of my new 7 × 12 room, rather she explained how things worked, and all the different storage places in the room. She had already left a fresh blanket, sheets and pillow in my room. She said she would get me some bottled water. Then she said she would wait outside while I freshened up, and she would walk me to the pie-car. I would later learn the pie-car was the pantry car running 24 × 7 on the train. She left me in my room and stepped out.

I entered the bathroom, stared at the mirror and asked the bewildered face staring back at me, "Do you have any idea what you are doing?" I shook my head, splashed some water on my face before the tears started again. I wiped my face and stepped down from the train.

She: Did you lock your room?

Me: No.

She: Always lock your room even if you are stepping out for a minute.

Me: (Thinking) Why would she say that?

We reached the pie-car. She introduced me to Mike, Greg and Jenny, who spared me the casual, "Hi, how you doing ..." and didn't wait for my answer. I mumbled, "Hi, I'm fine, how about you?" (Darn! Convent education again!)

Soon I would learn when someone says "Hi, how you doing?" You just say, "Hi, all good", even if you are dying.

Bea walked me back to my room and said that I could call her anytime. Also, if I needed grocery and other essentials, she and her husband would take me at 4 o'clock that afternoon. I said, "Great! That would be nice. Thank you".

As soon as she left me in my room, exhaustion, loneliness and a feeling of abandonment came over me. I fell on my bed and wept. And with tears flowing down in torrents, I fell asleep. 4 o'clock came and went. I woke up to a knock on my door. I opened it to find Bea with bags of stuff. Basic stuff. She said she had come at 4 o'clock. But I had been dead to the world. She also said, "Manna, even when you are inside the room, lock the door". I nodded.

She said that she and her husband would pick me up at 7 pm and take me out to dinner. I agreed. I had absolutely no appetite but accepted it merely to be in the company of some humans. I didn't want to be alone and be haunted by all that I had and was doing wrong in my life.

I went through the shopping bag, found milk, bread, eggs, butter, jam, coffee, juice, some cookies (biscuits), and a box of salad. I gobbled up some cookies and drank some juice. I hadn't had lunch as I was not sure I'd find the pie-car. I'm directionally challenged, you see. I couldn't remember if I got off the coach and walked left or right. I also didn't know if they would care enough to be kind. (Just so you know, they turned out to be my best friends on the show).

When I stepped out at 7, I found in front of almost every coach there was a grill setup and groups of people around. Drinking, laughing, talking ... just having fun. Bea and Tom were ready for me in their truck. We had a pleasant dinner. They asked about my home and my children and tears rolled down even though I didn't want it to. They reassured me that it was going to be difficult but I would soon settle and have a great time.

Tom and Bea were the angels God sent to help my transition into a new life. With that thought I went to bed. A few more days went by, acquainting with the routine of rising, going to bed, breakfast, lunch, dinner and above all preparing for the class – one classroom, 16 students and one teacher. Sounds easy perhaps for a regular teacher. It was different for me. I had seven different grades and all at different levels. Just when I thought I was getting the hang of it, I started hearing new jargons. My new vocabulary now included load-in, load-out, wagons, boxes, forklift and many more. I was finding it difficult to keep up. I tried to watch and listen closely and figure it out myself. What I gathered was we were ready to "take the show on the road". The first show of the tour would premier at The St. Pete's Times Forum (now Amalie Arena). The show kicked off for the years 2005 to 2007 December season. The show was put together and all the people had a camaraderie of which I was not a part. Truth be told, I didn't know how to fit in. Half the time, it was like living in the Biblical Tower of Babel. So many languages, and everyone had someone to talk to in their own language. Except for me. I wished to meet someone who could speak either Tamil, or Malayalam, or I could even manage Hindi. But my search was in vain.

It was one such day when I was almost going to give up hope that I spotted a forklift heading my way. I stepped aside and glanced at the driver. Oh! My heart pounded so hard. He must be from South India for sure. I walked towards him with a smile. He too started beaming warmly. I couldn't stop myself before I said, "Indian?" I think we are the only clan in the entire world who would start a conversation with that warm-kindred spirit. I was still smiling and elated when he replied, "¿Cómo estás?" I nearly died. You know how you want the earth to open and swallow you, or you want suddenly to become invisible??? I said, "I'm so sorry I thought you were an Indian". The guy kept grinning and spoke for the next 60 seconds at least. I picked up the word "maestro" and in the midst of gesticulating I also figured something like "When I was a kid, I went to a school myself". While I stood there tongue-tied, he continued with great excitement and was now pointing to the cafeteria. Inviting me for a cuppa? I wasn't sure but I switched on my flight mode; I bid a hasty retreat, pointing to my watch indicating I had some important things to do. My ears were burning just as much as his eyes were lit up and I kind of imagined he was asking me over for coffee. I tumbled along to my classroom and sat down on my chair while waiting for my students. Later that day, this man was again at the door of my classroom, the same grin, the same sparkle in his eyes. This time he was there to pick up his child who was 5 years old and his classes were getting over at 12.30. The son ran to him crying out, "Daddy". I was relieved. I had been so wrong; he was not trying to pick me up for coffee, he was just excited seeing the new teacher. I could handle that! As I continued my life there, I realized, contrary to what I have been taught and what I believed, daddies and husbands could and would try to pick you up. And by the time I learned that,

I had become adept at handling such overtures. So, any hope I had of finding my "folks" was soon crushed. I wouldn't ever be seeing anyone from my nation. A week flew past in Tampa. On one side, there was the hustle and bustle of the show … the practices, the schedules, the production department, the wardrobe, lights, sounds, everyone buzzing with activities. We were about to get on the road, after a month of being in Tampa. Suddenly all around me, I kept hearing words like get rolling, during the run, crew change, "haul, haul route, animal walk, porters, wagons, wagon tongues, lot set up, animal tents, dumpsters for the train yard and animal compound" – all phrases which slowly I would begin to experience and understand. But on that day, I was overwhelmed at the load of ignorance I had. Although there was an orientation for the entire troupe, there never was anything really that made sense to a teacher, who was completely disconnected with the show itself. While each department is addressed on what is expected of them, the school is never mentioned at any of the meetings. I used to feel offended at the beginning. Later, I began to realize that it was a completely independent entity and I had to run it on my own. I had to make my own decisions, make my lesson plans, conduct exams and focus on education for anyone under the age of 18. I was the Principal, HOD, subject specialist, all rolled into one. It didn't matter whether they could speak or understand English, which obviously was the medium of instruction.

That night, I made a few calls – first, to my children. Then my friend who was my kind of a local guardian, in Boston, but would be my family and her home would be my home for the rest of my stay in the US. When I called my children, I told them I was inside my train room. (It took me several months before I could say I'm back "home" from work!) I told them that after a couple of weeks, we would be moving to Orlando. They had a hundred questions. Did you eat? What did you eat? How will you sleep? Is there an AC? What about the bathrooms? Where is your school? I answered everything with a lot of precision, except when it came to the question about the school. I said I really didn't know where the classes were going to be held. I would find out when I got to the Arena. I had been told to take the 8 am shuttle bus that left the train. One of them asked me, "So your classes are going to be at the Arena?" "Yes", I replied.

The other one asked, "Are you prepared for the class?"

And I said, "No". I felt my heart sinking. I felt insecurity and fear grip my heart again. To change the topic, I asked them how their college was and reminded them that all this separation was temporary and they needed to complete their lessons before they went out for fun. Both boys were extremely talented, one an ace drummer and the other a natural event organizer and a basketball player. I fell asleep knowing that the next morning would be a new start, new hope and new experiences. I would be introduced to the class and parents the next day.

CHAPTER 14

I woke up early, thinking … "Today I begin afresh. I am going in for a job with no idea what to do". I boarded the shuttle bus the next morning, with a load of other people, all speaking different languages. It was more like a cackle of geese. I did not understand a single word. I found a vacant seat next to a young Chinese boy. He gave me a funny look and then said a lot in Chinese. He seemed agitated. I was scared. What did he tell me? How do I reply? This was not going to be easy. I just looked at him and said with a smile, "Monay, nee paranja oru aksharam polum enniku manasilayilla!" [Son, I didn't understand a single word of what you just said]. His mouth fell open for a second and then said something that sounded like, "Wo hen hao" [I would later learn it meant I am fine.]. He then sat looking out of the window for the rest of the ride. I had no idea what just transpired but whatever it was, he seemed ok. The bus was full of people from 20 odd nationalities, all excited about the sights they were seeing as we drove to the venue. Even in a crowded bus which seats probably 40, each had formed their own little native groups to converse in. I sat there alone thinking in my native tongue. I've had a lot of self-talk during my early days at the circus. In about 30 minutes we pulled up into a huge area filled with wagons with the logo of the show. People running helter-skelter, forklifts busy, Harlens (a tractor-like vehicle used for hauling heavy cargo) and then I saw a line of elephants walking towards a huge building in a line – one holding the tail of another. I counted, one, two, three, four … nine, ten, eleven, twelve. Two tiny ones were the eleventh and the twelfth. They were almost frolicking. It made me smile. I have seen elephants at temple festivals in Kerala. A maximum of three or four. But twelve? I was tempted to follow them when I heard my name being called, "Manna!" I swung around and came face to face with Mr. Jack. "Good morning, Mr. Jack", I said with a nervous smile. He didn't wish me back. He seemed stressed. "Come on, let me walk you over to the school room. They are all waiting for you", he said. I prepared my best charming smile for the little ones I had met in Detroit. I had even planned to tell them stories about India and my childhood and school. "You will be meeting the parents too", he added. My smile froze and my heart sank. Dealing with four students all under 10 years was a piece of cake. But parents? I prayed, "Lord, let them understand English, Malayalam, Tamil, or even Hindi". We were at a secluded building. I could hear voices of people jabbering. We opened the door and entered. And there I stood rooted, holding my folder close to my chest like an armour. More than 30 pairs of eyes stared at me. I recognized one or two faces. One was on his mother's lap. One rolled his eyes … the eye roller.

The GM Jack came forward and introduced me to the group. He really tried to make me sound like a super teacher. No one seemed convinced. At the end of that meeting, I realized I would have 18 students. Most of them were from the inner city of Chicago. School dropouts but ace acrobats. They spoke English alright. But I couldn't understand a word. Their slang and their accent were very foreign to me. What had I gotten myself into! They were big tall boys who were age-wise appropriate for Grades 11 and 12 but had never crossed the primary level. How do you take a 11th-grade lesson and teach someone at a 4th-grade level? This was a completely different ball game. This in itself was going to be a circus with me as the single performer doing many acts in one show.

Fear of failure, the feeling of incompetency, the attitude of unfriendliness from most didn't help me either. I blabbered who knows what … and unsuccessfully tried my Indian charm and went back to my room as a beaten soldier. I would have two years of this rigorous exercise. Would I last that long? I had to, I had no choice, did I? I was not willing to accept defeat. I was determined to teach, win them over and stay. I was not ready to walk away from that unusual place with my tail between my legs. That stoic determination is what gave me the gumption to stay on. Today I am so glad I did. How much it has changed me! How beautifully I have evolved! How different my perception of the world has become! I have realized that the world doesn't revolve around me, instead I drift around adapting, adjusting to the world around me.

It was January 2005, the date of the premier; the show was fully formed and was premiering at the State Fair Grounds, Tampa. The opening of the new show, the 135th edition, was at the St. Pete's Times Forum at Tampa. We played from the 5th of January to the 9th at the said location. The classroom moved from the Fair Grounds to the Arena. During this time, the books arrived for the students; the stationery was all stocked up. I also learned how to pack and move the school box from one place to another. There were two school boxes. It carried all the things needed for a classroom. Suddenly I was thinking of the demands and complaints of teachers back home about the lack of resources.

The box was about 6' high × 5' wide × 3' deep. I had two such boxes. One had doors on both sides, front and back. The other had doors on one side like any normal cupboard. Into these boxes went all the books of the students, craft materials, stationery for each child, laptops, printers, copiers, a small refrigerator, a microwave, and even a coffee maker. Both the boxes had to be tightly packed with Styrofoam if necessary so it doesn't move when in transit. They also had wheels, so the team who helped with load-in and load-out could roll these out into wagons.

At the end of every week, I had to pack everything into the boxes and secure them tightly and get them ready for the next move. The first thing I did every week in a new town was to open the box and transform the room allotted in the Arena to a school. Some rooms were carpeted and had good furniture. It usually would be a banquet hall that had to be a school room that week. In some cities, we would get something a little bigger than a cubicle.

The last thing I did in every city was pack "the school" into the two huge boxes. I stood there puzzled. It was easy to pull it out and set the room. However, while packing it all back, I always found there was no room for the very same stuff that came out of it. Somehow, I made sure it was secure enough and wouldn't fall off during the run. This I think was the most difficult task for me. The physical labour of lifting, carrying stuff and packing it all tightly. It was a herculean task. I have never ever in all the years of my life done anything even remotely close to it. Back home I had people at my beck and call. That thought didn't help and childishly just drew me into feeling sorry for myself. Honestly, on some days, I just stuffed everything into the box and hoped it wouldn't pop open and be strewn all the way to the next town. The students were still in the transitional stage and were not yet ready to help. "It's her job, let her do it" was their attitude. I somehow would manage to cram everything into the two boxes and head out to my room on the train.

Every new town started with my going to the Arena early enough to find the school room. I remember walking all over the Arena in circles looking for the school room. I would walk around looking for a sign that said "School". It was like a treasure hunt. Some places would have three floors and after looking through all the rooms, I would be exhausted and still wouldn't have found the room. As it usually would be very early in the morning, I did not usually find any Arena staff either to ask if they knew where I could find the school room. Our own staff would all be sleeping because their load-out would have finished only by 4 am. Even if you did find someone and asked if they knew where the school was, they would look at you strangely and answer, there's no school here, the circus starts today. I never bothered to explain further. Obviously, it was someone who came, did their job and went home. Each one carried on with their work, focused and unconcerned about anything else. Finally, there would appear someone who would know something about the school and circus. They are most of the time very excited and enthusiastic about the show and would be gushing about the Greatest Show on Earth. I heard some of it, the rest just blew right over my head. My first school day at any Arena was chaotic. I would have to arrange the room in a way that it enabled all the students, all grades, all age groups and all kinds of subjects to be able to "learn" something. No one seemed to be in a hurry to help me either. I could feel frustration rising within me and the flood gates would soon open. I had to stay calm and figure it all out … one step at a time. Somehow, I saw through the day and took the evening shuttle back to the train and my room. When I got there, I would see that the train was empty except for the few train crew. All the others would be at the Arena getting ready for the show.

CHAPTER 15

I remember the first day at the Arena when I had to "create" a school room from scratch. By the time I reached my room on the train I was exhausted. I had never felt so inept ever in my life – not even when I was stranded in London with no passport. I lay on the bed tears rolling down and unbeknownst to me a prayer rose up from deep within ... "Lord, Bend me, but please don't break me". The prayer my father had used his entire life – from when he walked his way from Burma to India during the Second World War, until the day he died. That one liner prayer always filled me with an energy, a courage then and it still continues even today. With that prayer on my lips, I fell asleep. (This story is included at the end of the book as the last chapter, "Bent, Yet Unbroken".)

I woke up early next morning, determined to teach. Determined to win them over. Determined to make a difference.

Task 1: Teach the over-13 years to write their names – on a straight line, in neat print. All the others will have work assigned to do on their own.

I walked into the classroom and said, "Good Morning".

No response. Just indifferent looks. I said, "I'm thinking of dividing the class into two". Immediately murmurs of disagreement arose from the big boys, which was emulated without hesitation by the little ones.

"But", I continued ... "the seniors will make the decision". Now I got a look of interest. I waited. One boy said, "We don't know the grades, so you do it".

I said, "That's ok ... you guys decide the best fit ... since you have all been seeing each other for a month now. The grades are my problem".

They started talking among themselves. I picked the one who I figured was leading the pack and gave him a paper and pen. Then, I sat down on a chair, pretending to flip through the pages of a random textbook lying there.

It was amazing to watch them work. There were siblings, twins, blacks, whites, browns. So, the discussions involved making each group mixed. The leader said, "Let's split the twins and siblings". In fact, one boy said with a grin, "You better put me and Ralph in separate groups, or we will be goofing around all the time".

That is when I knew I had won their respect! In 15 minutes, the list was ready. Then I said, "Now, get into your groups and then write down five questions to ask me. Things you want to know about me".

This was fun ... lots of laughter. One boy, 17 years, asked me, "If you were single would you date me?"

My Indian conditioning kicked in. "No", I said firmly, but with a smile, "That would be inappropriate". There was a lot of laughter.

They laughed because it was funny.

I laughed because I had their attention.

Task 1 accomplished!

After school hours, I would walk into the Arena and find an insignificant corner to watch the rehearsals. The elephants, the tigers, the globe of steel with the motorbikes, the acrobats, the jugglers, the trapeze artists, the riders on some beautiful horses from Kazakhstan, the dainty and elegant dancers, and the booming voice of the ring master narrating flawlessly and cuing each act. As I watched, I was thinking why the big fuss? It was just OK, not great, and certainly not the greatest. My limited knowledge of the running or life of the circus did not appreciate that it was a rehearsal and everyday was the fine tuning and an impeccable show would be on the road in no time.

The acrobats were mostly my students, agile and so skilful, and I soon began to form a new kind of respect for them. They were hard workers, loved what they were doing and wanted to excel. I started feeling proud that I knew them.

With every passing day, I began to see the show take form and shape. The Greatest Show was being created and I was privy to it in an indirect and unexpected way.

The joy of a creator, an artist, the production team, the wardrobe, the lighting and sound – all fell into place. Towards the end of the month, this spectacular show would well be on the road, entertaining thousands of people across the United States. It took me time to realize how I was part of a huge project. I may not have been in the ring, but my role was crucial by the laws laid down by the Department of Education (DOE). If a person under 18 were to perform, they would have to attend school for a minimum of 3 hours per day. The frequent visits from the DOE could cost the circus a lot, if things were not in place, like the curriculum, the attendance, the lesson plans. They usually gave very little notice before their visit. The acts involving under-18-year-olds could be pulled off from the show as a violation of the right to education. So, while thousands may come and watch the glam and glitter, silently behind the scene was I, in one sense, responsible for making sure the performing kids were in school and doing their job.

One thing that happened week after week while on the circus was the interviewing. As part of the publicity, just before we got to a new city, there would be a call which either took my story for the local newspaper or to set up the time for a TV channel to come visit the school and see the school and take the story of the "Circus School". Initially, I was very excited but then it became a routine.

I clearly remember the first interview. It was December 2004. The Tsunami had hit the southern parts of India. So as an Indian just to get out on the streets would invariably bring a question from total strangers, "Are you from India? How is your family back home?" I was pleasantly surprised. Although the Tsunami had not directly affected *any* of my immediate family or friends, I loved the attention. Well, I did milk it a bit. I spoke about my son back home and also said the other son was in the US. The journalist immediately asked me if she could interview the son who was in the US. I said, "Sure, but let me give him a heads up". Soon I called my son who is infamous for his spontaneous sarcasm and wit, that I had to warn him that this was serious. He laughed and agreed. I was more nervous worrying about what would come out of his mouth, than what I was being asked. I was new to the job, and so if they asked me how I would hold classes, my answer would have been blank. I wonder what if I had said something like, "I don't know what I am going to do!". Thank God for the gift of the gab, I pulled off my part smoothly. Later, they called my son and I was waiting anxiously to hear what he had said. But my son's response was, "You can read about it in tomorrow's paper". I was nervous and jittery throughout the day. I grabbed the newspaper the next day and here's what it said: George's (I was then using the surname George) older son, a student in Indianapolis, said, "I am proud of my mother; even if many people in India have never heard of teachers for the circus, she dares to try. She's not the kind of person who would stick around if she doesn't like it", said Geo. "And if she doesn't like something, she moves on". Is this what he thinks of me? Is that a good thing? I was left wondering what he really meant. But then that's him. Long after he has said something, you will be wondering what he really meant! My delivery during each interview varied. It would depend a lot on how I felt on that particular day. It also would depend on how the interviewer posed the questions. But mostly it would depend on how I was feeling in terms of my personal life or my professional life. The same story took different hues based on these unpredictable changes.

CHAPTER 16

I woke up one morning excited. This was the day that I was going to experience my first train journey. I knew I wasn't supposed to cook on the move. I quickly made some comfort food (read as Indian food) and stored it in the fridge. I went to the washer to do a load. I found it locked. I didn't know what to do. Maybe they forgot to give me the key to the washer. I called Bea. She picked up but it sounded like she was busy. But still she politely asked me what I needed. I said, "The washer is locked, you didn't give me the key". She laughed, "Yes the washer is locked and it will be opened in Orlando". I felt sheepish but thanked her. (I would later learn the washers will remain closed during the run to save the stored water.) When the train is stationary, we are directly connected to the water supply.

Mental note: I must try to do my laundry the day before the train run.

I settled down to read and while I was reading, the train moved slowly. I panicked. The people in adjoining rooms were not in. But then it stopped suddenly. I didn't know if I should go out and check. But I sat tight. Just then there was a knock. I opened to find Bea. She said they were "putting the train together". So, the flat beds (the ones that carry the wagons, the animal cages and the concession cars) would all be assembled, and connected to the coach cars. "There will be a lot of back-and-forth movement", she continued to explain the putting together. She also gave me bungee cords to secure my TV, fridge, and boxes on the top bunk. "If not secured, they could move, fall off or be damaged during the run", she added.

As she hurried out of my room to complete her duties she added, "Don't miss the view from your window as you will see acres and acres of orange orchards on either side of the tracks".

I thanked her and immersed myself in the reading. I was jolted a few times by coaches coupling and finally the train moved to a track ready to move. For those curious minds, we own the train but not the locomotives. Those are from different railroads – Amtrak, BNSF Railway, CSX Transportation, Norfolk Southern Railway, Union Pacific Railroad to name a few.

Finally, the coaches got noisy and people started coming back to their "homes". The chatter outside my door made no sense to me at all. It was all gibberish. One thing I understood from their tones, they were all happy. Perhaps all were looking forward to the train ride like me.

The train pulled out and I began my first circus train

journey. In general, I loved train rides. This was different. I could stay in my pjs; I could lounge on my bed, prop up my pillow and look outside through the only window in that room.

As soon as we left the Tampa city area, we passed people waving from either side of the tracks yelling out, "Thank you" and "See you soon". The coming and going of the circus was an event for people in the towns. The landscape outside started to change. It was like watching scenes change in a movie. The urban side was left behind and we started seeing more rural areas. Then slowly I started seeing scenes which were more like paintings.

Imagine miles and miles of dark green small shrubs dotted with oranges. I ventured out on to the vestibule (what I would later refer to as my patio) and took it all in. It was breathtaking, perhaps a part of the Garden of Eden. I took lots of pictures. I even took some videos. After a couple of hours, I needed a bathroom break. I went back to my room. And then it happened! I wasn't sure if I could use the bathroom on the run. The washers were locked, right? So maybe I shouldn't use the toilet too. And I really wanted to go. I mean really, badly wanted to go. I sat tight. The orchards didn't distract me. I squirmed around, crossed my legs, uncrossed them. Do I just pee? A little pee on the track won't matter, will it? Yet what if someone finds out it was Indian pee ... It will just confirm "the dirty third world" image for them. I wanted to cry ...

I missed my country. We just go when we want to, don't we? My mind floated to our Indian railways. How laid back we are ...! When in a difficult situation, it is unbelievable how my mind conjures up a thousand near-impossible scenarios that are of no use. In fact, it just adds on to the already existing torture.

Finally, after what seemed like an eon, the train came to a halt. It did the same back and forth and jolts and stopped. Every jolt was a threat to peeing on myself. In a few minutes, there was a knock. I opened and found Bea. "You doing alright? Did you enjoy the ride?" I didn't answer her. Instead ...

Me: When can I pee?

She looked shocked: "Poor you! You can use the bathroom anytime!"

I dashed into the bathroom, leaving her at the door.

I came out and she was laughing. I said I was afraid of ruining the tracks. She asked me to get down and look under the coach. Every toilet had a tank, the septic tank so to say. I may have looked confused, because she added, "We have tankers come that empty every tank in the mornings; yours would have been empty" she added with a wicked smile.

It made sense. Why didn't we have this system back in India? The busy tracks were more like septic tanks. This was an unforgettable train ride on many counts. The smooth ride, the panoramic view from the comforts of my room, and the agony of holding my pee in for what seemed like ages. However, it was just a couple of hours. I was beginning to get hungry. I pulled things out of the refrigerator and made a plate of my favourite meal – rice, dal, thoren and fish fry (rice + lentils + vegetable sautéed with coconut + fish fry), the ultimate comfort food. I heated it in the microwave and sat down to have my first lunch on the train. It tasted like home. I missed my sons. I looked at the time; it must be about 2 am in Chennai. I had to wait for them to wake up and then call.

The first day in Orlando was a free day. It was a Monday and I knew that I didn't have to go to work until Wednesday. These two days were used to put the show up in the Arena. Load-out and rigging happens almost immediately. I had none of those responsibilities. All others headed out to the Amway Arena to set up the show, rehearse and life moved on. I had not yet made any friends and I wasn't sure how to go out and do sight-seeing. So, I just stayed in my room planning the week's lessons for all the students. At least I will be prepared with my job.

Later I kicked myself for not going to the Disney World where tickets were on a discount for circus employees. There were two reasons why I did not want to venture out.

1. Financial constraints, too many commitments to set aside money for fun

2. No friends as yet. Who wants to go to Disney World alone and spend a day?

Both these scenarios changed over time and I did go to Disney Land both in Orlando and Anaheim.

CHAPTER 17

Train rides have always been a time for reflection and introspection. I always let my thoughts fly out unfiltered. After all, no one was there to interrupt. Coming from a very conservative family where patriarchy was at its peak, it was a huge adjustment. I had a problem when people treated me with respect and accepted me for who I was. It was confusing to receive the respect. It was hard to believe it was real. When was the last time I was just me and not someone's daughter/mother/sister/partner? Don't get me wrong, I loved all of those roles. I still do.

Even if separated/divorced the woman was always "the woman who used to be married to …" Years after the marriage breaking, there is always someone asking, "So where is …" (referring to the ex) or "How is …" I used to rant and rave and respond aggressively. My years of self-imposed exile got me to a place of forgiveness and serenity within me. Joy returned. I could now answer, "He's doing well in his home, I suppose".

In my culture, I think the woman has some traction

when and if she is in her own home, as long as the parents are around, after which she is owned by everyone else. Once she enters her husband's home, the story doesn't change. More people are waiting to pounce on the new bride to teach her the ropes. Nothing can be done without their consent. When you wake up, when you go to bed, when you eat, what you eat are all mechanically executed through others. Not going to church called for punitive measures, often accompanied by a threat of the doomsday. According to many, listening to music, watching a movie, even reading a book are all worthless activities of an irresponsible lazy woman. How I survived the early years of a marriage which was a huge pride and joy for my parents, I cannot imagine. I had to be everything I was not. In the meantime, there were many women in my new home who thought I was a poor catch. There were proposals from better educated girls, more suitable matches, they reminded me whenever opportunity presented itself. To be fair, these were said in the sweetest of tones and in passing. That was a shock too. From a home where I was the apple of the eye, to a place to be constantly reminded of how worthless I was and not domesticated enough was a wound inflicted time and again. Did I react? No. I sought to please everyone, by complying with the requirements. I tried to buy their affection with material things. They were not bad people. They were from another age and time and didn't know better. This brings back a lot of memories from my childhood home. What a joy it was to be in the presence of my brothers and parents. Laughter and joie de vivre all day every day. The fights with siblings and always managing to look the victim … are all a matter of pleasant memories and the payoff for being the only girl in the midst of four brothers.

I grew up in a home where summer holidays meant board games and card games. My father would bring all five of us around and play during the day. His reasoning was to prevent the boys from getting restless and wandering out. Their friends were welcome to come home and join too. We would play for hours, amidst heated arguments, friendly competitions and mean jibes. Those were the best memories of my childhood summer vacations. Thus, when I became a mother, it was with no malice or thoughts of anything vile that I carried a pack of cards with me for my kids so that I could keep them indoors. Both had severe allergies to the soil and insects in that town. After every summer holiday, I ended up taking them on several visits to the doctor for treatment for skin eruptions. When this happens, I am on my own to deal with the eczema of not one child but both!

One day, "Oh! Great! Teaching your kids to play cards and gamble at such a young age, uh?", a sarcastic reprimanding tone intruded on the peaceful fun-filled room. The games we played were memory or bluff. I was a bad mom for teaching kids to play cards. By that time,

I was 7 years into the marriage and I had learned to ignore these comments. Keeping my children from playing out in the mud, getting bitten by bugs and developing skin eruptions became my focus. We didn't live there permanently. We were there for a week to 10 days. If I didn't take care of my children, then I would have several months of dermatologist visits on my hands after the so-called vacation. Although I belligerently ignored the "bad mom" comments, somewhere it left a dent. Maybe I am a bad mom.

Children witness all these dynamics. However little, they see, they understand, they form their own set of rules and regulations to use when they grow up. Most of the time we parents do not teach them. They watch and learn. I am not too sure what they have picked up and what they have left out of their own lives. I have no idea how they processed all of this. Now when I look at them, they seem to have done well. But for me, what did not endure the test was my marriage itself. The notes I had made in my head about what a marriage should be were not in sync with what was happening in my life. My father was a partner to my mom, a companion, and a provider. He was perfect. I say this knowing well that there is no perfect parent. But you know what I mean. He had time for me. He played, nurtured, talked, respected and even gave me the greatest gift ... the love for books. The best companion he had ever introduced me to was books. He loved, respected, cherished and provided companionship to my mother, which is why I believed that all marriages were like that.

Once the initial excitement and newness of my marriage wore down, little by little I began to feel a sense of I-do-not-belong. I could never say or do anything right. I was not heard. I started becoming the voiceless one merging into the nothingness. Once my father slipped into his own world via Alzheimer's I had no one. Well, maybe, it isn't entirely true. I had no one who would hear me out fully before doling out advices. I started moving into a cozy mental space. Actually, it had two compartments – one for the world and one for me. And we all know living a lie will eventually get you nowhere. Therefore, there came a time when I had to keep one of those compartments and let go of the other. I did think of the repercussions. I even sought counsel from a renowned counsellor. Interestingly, his comment was to build up a support system for myself before I let go of the marriage, or it was going to be very difficult, he advised. It was not until after the separation that I began to feel the impact of those words. Then began my trudge through a road less travelled – a road where I did not find many fellow travellers. It may as well have been the wilderness.

I was once watching a movie, don't remember the name. It was a train where one end had caught fire. The train was going at a tremendous speed. One way to salvage what was left of it was to detach the burning damaged part from the rest of the train. That's what I did. I detached the part that was a raging destructive fire, gathered what I could salvage of my life and moved far away. When you are face to face with a catastrophe, the only thing on your mind is survival. There is no time to weigh the pros and cons. Your brain tells you to get out as fast as you can and later do damage control if you feel like it. It was like the tumblers in the circus. Just jump through one hoop through to the next and the next. In the midst of all this, I would suddenly, even if briefly, land on a padded mattress, a respite – just enough time to catch my breath back.

It was then that I remembered what the wise man had told me. Build a support system around you before you choose the rough road. And I thought those words were just something he had to say. I had not built any buffers. I had no padded mattress waiting to catch me when I landed. I found myself completely alone, perhaps some crumbs here and there that fell off the table of some banquet. I am not ungrateful. These crumbs did help me get back some energy. But looking back, I wonder how I traversed such a treacherous and arduous road.

Some days, it seemed like there was no end to the onerous journey.

Some days, I've wanted to give up.

Some days, I had a surge of energy for no apparent

reason and was sure I would succeed. These surge days were few and far between. But it was better than a steady feeling of ineptness. If I were to survive, I realized I had to practice the three Ds …: detachment, distancing, dispassion.

Thus, this trajectory took me some 14000 km (8500 miles), approximately, away from my home and everything that was familiar. That's how far I needed to be, to heal. On retrospection, I can see that it is with a reason that I walked alone in certain stages of my life. I realized that I it was an utter waste of my time if all I did was hold pity parties. The sooner I focused on covering the distance, the faster I could come out of it.

It is on this road that I met The Greatest Show.

It is on this road that I discovered traits I did not know I had.

It is on this road that I learnt that walking alone didn't mean being lonely.

It is on this road I found the difference between religiosity and spirituality.

It was my road to Damascus.

The last job revealed to me that I was daring. I worked in a circus – an unbelievable and unheard-of achievement. I was the only Indian to have been on the unit it its century-and-a-half run!

CHAPTER 18

I need to get back to the circus. The show and its glitter and glam aside, there was a whole different world with the circus – in fact, the hub of the show, I would say. Putting the show together is a herculean task. There are a million details that go into it: timing, precision, maximum work with minimum supervision and above all accountability that tops the list. It is interesting to watch how when the time comes for load-in or load-out, there are people geared up and ready for work. There is the train crew, who take care of anything and everything to do with the train – for example, keeping the electricity running, ensuring the availability of water or maintaining the room temperatures optimal with minimum disruptions. In order for this to happen, the train crew must be on their feet, ready to go as soon as the train stops. The train is "put away", as the term goes, in three parts. The animal cars are disconnected from the train to a spot nearest to the Arena to allow minimal walking through the busy streets. However, there are places where the "Animal Walk" is an event. These usually happen in places where the city is circus friendly. So, the first part of the train is disconnected from the rest of the train. The next part would be the flatbeds. These carry the wagons, the company vehicles, forklifts and our beloved bus.

The bus was white in colour. The joke around it was that the buses that transported jailbirds from one place to another were the same colour. We tried protesting; we tried suggesting a bright doodle of sorts. But somehow it never happened. The flatbeds and the coaches are separated and again the flatbeds would be at a place where there is road access to roll the wagons off using a ramp and then pulled by the Harlens to the Arena. The wagons are numbered and each number would stand for a department or performer. So, when I see them being hauled, I always imagine my school boxes in one of them, carrying my school life and those of my students. It amazes me how my schoolroom travels with me from one city to another and how I start a new school in every city. How many teachers can say they have done it? If one box is not loaded or goes missing, that could hold up the entire show in the next city. And that would mean the reputation of the company, loss of money and a city full of disappointed people. I say this to impose the gravity of the role each and every person plays in the smooth running of the show. The last part is when the train with its 64 coaches is "put away" for the entire stay in that city.

Not all cities are circus friendly. Some of them are actually hostile. There are a lot of animal activists and rather than fight for a cause, their aim is to disrupt and create disarray for the animals and thus show the unhappiness of the animals. On the other hand, there are cities where they hold a brunch for the elephants. A banquet is laid for these princesses – fruits, vegetables and other goodies laid out on tables covered with satin, with frills and laces.

As for us, some cities are more interesting and exciting than some others. The excitement begins when we hear that the coaches are going to be split into parts and parked parallel to each other. What that means is when I step out of my room and on to my vestibule, my neighbour could be my best friend, and that means, a week's long partying, eating and cooking together. However, a boring week is when the track in the yard is long enough to park the train in one long line and needs no cut. This means my friend could be a mile away from me.

Once the locomotives are disconnected from the train, there is no power. The train crew led by the electrician then draws huge power cables and gets the entire train hooked up to the generator. Yes, we do have a generator car (an entire coach) which carries a generator providing power supply to the 300 people. A remarkable thing to be mentioned is how between losing power when the locomotives are disconnected and the power is hooked on, it takes just a few minutes. On a bad day posed by weather, or less hands or even the topography of the train yard, it took perhaps 30 minutes maximum. It is with military precision and discipline that this is done. I have always been proud of this team. Most worked and least appreciated department, I'd say.

Another sub-team walks through the coaches clearing garbage bags and replacing fresh ones. There are about four or five of them, who do this for the 64 coaches in a methodical and precise way. Huge dumpsters would be placed in every yard before we get there. These dumpsters are cleared every day. All these are done meticulously and it shows the efficiency and discipline of the crew.

There are people to clean common showers and toilets every day. If you think of the circus and the glam and glitter, remember, there is more to it. There is definitely a team working with no spotlight and glitter, but who are equally if not more important than those in the actual ring. The reason I say this is because if it weren't for them making the living conditions expedient, it would have made living difficult for those who go out there and make the circus happen. Therefore, if I haven't appreciated them then, as much as I should have, I do it now. And in retrospect I realize what a service they have been doing!

We had a waterman as I'd like to call him. As soon as the coaches were spotted, his job was to hook up the water pipes to the closest water hydrant (the parking of the train depends on the water hydrant too). He then walks from one end of the train to the other making sure that the tanks are all filled up. He cannot over-sleep, or take his own time doing this, because he is the water authority and you know how important water is. There was one time when the train was parked in a yard, and there was an overpass and the nearest water hydrant was on that bridge. Thus, for the whole week that we were in that town, this huge water hose hung from the bridge down to the train. It was not an easy task but the waterman got it done. Sometimes I had not even seen or considered these things, I just went about my life, never ever paused to think of the amount of effort that went behind getting the water to flow out of my faucet when I turned it on every morning.

The Greatest Show had not just one train and one unit. There were three units. They were the red, blue and gold. I was lucky enough to have been on all three at some point or the other. The red and blue were similar and had this mile-and-a-half-long train each. There were about 300+ people on each unit. The gold unit was much smaller, about a 100, and they moved around in charter buses or motor homes. If the distance was over 500 miles, they were flown into the next town instead of riding the charter buses. So, on any given day of the year, these three units would be crisscrossing the country. Most of the people on all the three units were friends or would have moved around from one unit to another at some point or the other.

I did too. I started out on the Red Unit and later moved to the Blue Unit. During one winter break, I was asked to take care of the school on the Gold Unit while they were waiting to hire a new teacher. Would I be able to claim that now I am the only teacher who worked on all the three units? I'm not sure about that, but I can dream on, can't I?

Did we all get together ever? Not really, but there had been a rare occasion or two when the Red and the Blue trains crossed each other. This was always such fun. There were a lot of buzz and preparation on both trains, because both units had friends on the other. Sometimes an announcement was made by the Train Masters on both trains as the trains approached each other. Everyone got out on the vestibule cheering, waving, screaming, hollering out to each other. You've got to be there to understand the emotion. It was such a happy joyous moment. The bond was warm and palpable. It was like meeting your dear one after years – except that the two trains will be speeding past on parallel tracks and in opposite directions. I remember, once, the Train Masters of both the units coordinated with their respective railroads and they stopped next to each other briefly. The air filled with sounds of jubilation; friends greeting friends resounded all around. The feelings of camaraderie that erupted at moments like these were palpable. These are the small joys of an otherwise busy life.

While almost everyone used the time on the train run to recoup and rejuvenate for the new week, there were some who were working without actually "going" to work. They may be in the warmth/chill (depending on the weather) of their room, but would still be working. One such would be the Purchasing Manager. While I was there, it was my friend, BFF, who was the PM. Considering we were such good friends, we hardly found time to just hang out during the train run. This was because she would be getting things in order for the next town. Shenia would constantly be on the phone with vendors in the next town ordering things that were needed for performers, for the animal crew or the train crew. It always blew my mind how she would have everything ordered, delivered and ready by the time we got into the new town. Be it food for the big cats, shoes for the performers, special grains for the horses, the waste disposal company, the dumpsters in the yard, or even ordering the books for the school kids, she had it all done. She was hard working and efficient. And this super woman was also passionate about baking. She would bake goodies like cookies to cupcakes and she would have that ready in her office for people to pick up. She also would find time to hang out with me for her favourite butter chicken and parotta or an early morning breakfast of scrambled eggs, bacon and sausage, which we carried out to the vestibule with our coffee and had our breakfast, and watched the scenic view rush past us as we caught up on our gossip. Oh! Come on! Don't judge us. We trusted each other not to take it to the third person. Also don't we all go home and talk to our families about what happened at work? This was my home and she was a member of my family. It was also a time for a lot of laughter and tears. We all have our joys and sorrows which we carry with us to work and bring it back. If we didn't have our personal wailing walls, how would we have managed? We were each other's wailing wall.

Most Sundays are our closing day in a town. We had a late start. We used that time to go for a sumptuous breakfast. She loved her pancakes and syrup with bacon. I loved my breakfast skillet with sausages, cherry tomatoes, baby spinach, bell peppers and an over easy egg on top. I had a special way of eating it. I would start at the sides, finish everything off and leave the egg for the last. I would start eating the sides, that's the whites, and when what is left is a mouthful, I would scoop it and drop it in my mouth. I close my eyes and feel the yolk explode in my mouth. Just one word ... ecstasy!! Shenia sits there watching me do it every Sunday and laughs in amusement.

We also did our weekly grocery together. Since she had her own vehicle, she helped me do my grocery shopping at leisure. I would be back from the store loaded with stuff, and she would drop me right up to my doorstep. In fact, we would first drop her stuff off because she had more stuff than I did. She used to bake for the entire crew, that's a couple of hundred people – no small matter that! Once all her stuff was unloaded, she drove me to my doorstep – such love and consideration. I kept the best for the last ... office politics and gossip. Oh! come on! We all do it, so don't raise your eyebrows.

I would be in class and juggling with my students and their subjects when she would walk past the classroom with a certain "look" on her face. Just that look or sometimes the walk told me I needed to step outside right at that moment. There she would be hidden from the eyes of the students, bursting with the "news". Now here is what we do ... I get only the headlines. The details would be divulged at Starbucks, Chipotle or Red Lobster later that day. Those who know these places will understand that it is proportional to the depth of the "news". But we used to celebrate every laughter and how we would laugh! I miss those moments but I am extremely glad and proud of those memories.

Our trips to Walmart, mostly as part of her official shopping, always ended up with something insanely funny. Like the time we were in an aisle picking up dry fruits, the store was fairly empty. All of a sudden, there was this loud rumble from the next aisle. Flatulence!!! The kind of release like he had been waiting for a quiet corner to let it all out. We ran from the area fearing the stink that could soon float across to the next aisle. We didn't see the person. I always wish I had peeked but at that moment it was run as far as you can. That laughter called for a celebration. Our life was not all fun and laughter.

Once, we were in Denver, Colorado. The altitude is pretty high and those who go there from lower altitudes, if not careful, do have issues like dizziness, headache, nausea, breathlessness and so on. We, as a unit, were advised to take in plenty of water. This is overlooked because Denver being a colder place we forget to take sufficient water. We went about our business, a tad lethargically, but she was doing her job with the usual efficiency and I was going about mine. During the wee hours of a morning, I got a call. I picked it up. It was Shenia. She said, "Hey I am going to the hospital, not feeling very good". I asked her how she would get to the hospital. She told me that she was driving. I said, "No! wait. I'm coming with you". I jumped up, changed out of my pjs, and was on my way with her. She seemed a little out of sorts. Her driving was not as smooth as always. I asked her if she was doing alright and her response was, "I am not able to see properly". My heart jumped to my throat. Here I was in Denver, Colorado, 2 am, in a van with my best friend, who was driving with poor vision and feeling unwell. I felt I had made the biggest mistake. I should have woken up someone else and at least informed that we were going to the hospital. What if she lost control and the van rolled off the slopes? Hurtling down the Rockies was not one way I had envisaged my end. But my wild imagination came to a stop as we pulled up in front of the hospital. She was immediately attended to and she was hooked up with some IV and I had a spare bed on which I could rest. I saw her settle down and she said that she was doing better. I got up to go to the restroom, and all of a sudden, I felt the room swirl and the next thing I knew, I was on the floor repeating that I needed a doctor. It may have been a brief spell of dizziness, because as I came around my friend was screaming for help and pulling off all the tubes attached to her. I got help too. We still laugh at the funny change of scene at the hospital. The nurses who otherwise would have had a peaceful night had an eventful one. One of them said, "The circus is in town!" To this day, I wonder what that was supposed to mean! Nevertheless, I am grateful for Shenia in my life.

This next story is probably the most bizarre one. We had both finished early and had planned to head to the grocery store and get some dinner. Just as we were leaving the Arena, the GM (Jack) called Shenia on the phone. He had a certain tone of urgency. He said, "If you are still around the Arena, don't leave, I need you to drive someone back to the train". We made a detour in the parking lot and headed to the loading area. There we saw the manager with two other people trying to hold one person up. He seemed weak and almost ready to collapse. I thought this was going to be a repeat of the incident with Cynthia (wait for that story). But before we could ask or say anything, this person was dumped on to the back seat of the van. The manager said, "Take him back to the train; he is too drunk to be on duty". Both Shenia and I were quiet – a drunk completely smashed at the back of our van! We drove in silence. I was scared, not really knowing what to do with a drunk. After some time, there was a slight groan from the back of the van, almost in agony. My friend looked through the rear view and yelled out, "No, No, No! We are almost there!" It was too late. He had pulled out his weenie and eased himself on to the floor mat in the van. I was in shock. But my friend was furious and was cussing out. She keeps her car clean and pristine. When we reached the train, she called for help and asked that he be dragged out. She stopped by a coach which had the facility to use a power hose to wash the van down. I walked back to my room without a word, far from the fury of my friend and the shock of this behaviour. It took us a couple of days to laugh about it. And when we finally laughed, it was until we almost peed on ourselves. The circus life! Never a dull moment!

CHAPTER 20

Let me switch gears here. We all had ways and means to maintain a certain amount of normalcy. Don't get me wrong; we were "circus normal". This I say in a good way, not in a negative way. I shouldn't even have to explain myself here. But knowing there are those who must define everything by normalcy, I thought it best to define my normalcy. We threw a party when happy; we threw a party when sad; we threw a party when angry. There were celebrations over birth and weddings; there was a party to drown one's sorrow at death or divorces. When we were down or felt on top of the world, we partied and were rallied by friends. Pretty much our world was filled with celebrations – a lesson the non-circus world can learn from. A bonhomie, crossing barriers of all kinds!

It was not easy to live in an environment like that, especially for someone like me. The world I came from had celebrations. It was so structured and predictable. A day, date and time always preceded a celebration. There was a structured agenda to the celebration. There were set places around the dining table; the host family would always have a rehearsed conversation in place. This, on looking back, may have been for my benefit. I was the one who run my mouth with no filter; I was the one who believed in conversations undiluted and unfiltered. But if you were in a "proper" home, that was unacceptable. There was always a person of importance at every celebration. Even for a birthday, the important person was not always the birthday boy/girl. It was a great uncle, a colleague of the father's, or even a religious head. Everything had to be kicked off by this VIP. I resented this on my birthdays. Why? Why? What were they celebrating? That's probably why I was left with the notion that I was not worth celebrating. And that's where I probably learned that I needed to take a step behind so someone else could be celebrated, even though rightfully it was my day.

Finally, I get a chance to see and live in this magical world, where all people are really equal. The venue for the party would be the same for all the three hundred plus people of this little town.

This is a place where I learned to look at people as people and not as the country they come from. This is where I learned that there were people who had Faith so strong that I began to doubt what I called Faith. This is where I realized that when people treated you well, it was because of who they were and not because of whose daughter/wife/sister/mother I was. It was very refreshing, once I learned to be comfortable with it. This is where I learned that people with different sexual orientations were just as human as I was. They laughed, they cried, they could be happy, get angry, or feel sad. They ate the same food as me. How can I not be grateful for these experiences!

I am yet to see a place where you have all of your being taken care of in a generic way. You want someone to pray with, there is that someone. You want someone to have a drink with, there is that someone. You want someone to read a book or discuss one with, there is that someone. You want someone to celebrate with, there is that someone. There is always someone around to make life better for you.

This was also a place where I learned that age was respected. There are people who have been there for over 40 years. I am sure they would have slowed down over the years. No one threw them away; they did not become redundant. They remained until they couldn't lift a straw and they themselves retired, or until ill health totally debilitates them forcing them to leave. I have seen young men and women who have stepped in to help the older person, even do his job sometimes, just so he can continue to be there. Where else does this happen? This is not a rhetorical question. It's a challenge question. Name one other place on Earth this happens … Exactly. Only at the circus will you find a glimpse into heaven. I was blessed to be privy to this amazing piece of heaven on Earth.

This one incident remains etched in my mind. It was during one of the load-ins. The train crew was working tirelessly, getting the wagons off the flatbeds and hauling them to the Arena. There was a lot of friendly jibing and jokes being thrown around. This time, the flat beds were parked right next to the coaches. I came out to the vestibule, to watch them work. It's not often that I can see this. As I stood there watching, one of them just slumped and fell to the ground between the coaches and flatbeds. This person was a heavy guy too. All came running to help him up. But he was gone. I don't even want to describe how he was dragged or hauled over from under the train to the ambulance. I watched the ambulance drive away. Tears streaming down my cheeks and my body shivering, I went back to my room. What had just happened??? I hoped against hope that he would be revived. The unit was pregnant with the shock and grief of having lost a member of this unique family. The show must go on … Because before you know it, there is the rigging, practices and the show looming ahead. I couldn't get rid of that scene from my mind. The students couldn't get rid of it. Just the previous week, our field trip had been with the Department of Transportation of the Unit. This gentleman had given rides to the students on the Harlens. I had created an opportunity for my students to get close to him and now he was gone.

Grief takes a while to settle down. Healing happens

faster when there is a closure. It was with this thought in mind that I approached the AGM and asked him if we could do a memorial service to honour him. What a beautiful service it was! We flew down his family, and they got to hear everything about the person who left us without a goodbye. The service was organized by us … the school. The AGM made a speech and as I later jokingly told him, "You should have been a minister" – a moving eulogy it was. My students spoke too. It gave us something to hold close to our hearts as a memory. Painfully beautiful.

CHAPTER 21

We were a city without a zip code. Yet, we carried all the essence of a city. We had the freedom, and yet were protected. A few months into the show and it was my birthday. No one knew my birthday and I didn't feel close enough to tell anyone that it was my birthday. I knew once again I would have to spend it alone and unnoticed. But before the big day arrived, I happened to have a conversation with one of my students. He said he would be 7 on the 25th. And I spontaneously said, "Oh! That would be two days after mine". I thought nothing much of it. But then in true circus style, it followed a certain communication network. And oblivious to me, there was a party brewing. As for me, as the day approached, my heart was sinking, getting more and more homesick, and even missed the celebration back home of which I had complained earlier. All the students had made cards for me. I knew the soon-to-be 7-year-old was the culprit. I felt like a 7-year-old myself and wanted to distribute sweets/chocolates in true Indian style. There were demands that there be no class that day as it was my birthday. I smiled remembering my school days when we did the same thing. It was just any reason to get out of lessons. Children world over are the same I thought and gave in to the request. By noon, Mia, one of the nursery teachers, dropped by. To my eyes she looked 18, and was pregnant. I always felt sorry for her. She was always tired. My motherly instinct stirred in me. She was not yet a friend, but we were friendly enough to exchange pleasantries. She walked into the class and found the students all over the place and doing fun stuff. Some were playing board games, some drawing, some painting, some doing crafts. She had never seen my class in such disarray. She seemed pleasantly surprised. "Oh! A fun day, is it?" she asked cheerily. "Oh! It's Ms. Manna's Birthday", the class chorused. I was embarrassed. She looked at me accusingly and said, "You never told me". She hugged me and wished me. My first hug on my birthday and probably the only one. I felt tears stinging my eyes. An overwhelming feeling of sadness came over me. My children had called me at midnight to wish. "So, this is pretty much my birthday celebration", I had told myself. She walked around the classroom, looked at the kids working and then left the class. The rest of the day went by quietly. By the end of the class, I had a ton of cards, all kinds of decorations with misspelt birthday wishes, and a bunch of happy students wishing everyday was my birthday.

I went back to my room and made myself a cup of

coffee, and sat down with my laptop. There were a bunch of e-cards. That's what we did those days, the first transition from store-bought real cards to digital greetings. (I miss those e-cards!) I sulked and asked myself what difference it would have made had I been back home in India? That's when I realized that it would have been the same. With both sons away at college, they would have done the same things – called at midnight, sent an e-card, and then … I told myself this was better. I went through each and every piece of paper the students had given me. I picked the best from each one and put it up on my tiny refrigerator and on the walls of my room. "Happy Birthday, Manna", I said out aloud. I hadn't wished myself that morning.

It must have been close to 10 pm and I was getting ready for bed when there was a knock on my door and Mia was calling out to me, "Hey, Manna, are you awake?" I opened the door and she said, "Come with me. I want to show you something". I hesitated. I made excuses. I've changed into my pjs, I'm feeling tired, I've a long day tomorrow – I came up with all that I could think of. She wouldn't take any of those. She said, "You can change into proper clothes or I'm going to drag you in your pjs". So, I changed and went with her. There was a whole coach for the circus band. The band was a group of extremely talented young men. And Mia's husband was part of it. I entered the coach and realized a loud noisy party was in progress. People were already drinking and eating. As soon as I entered, all of them shouted out "Happy Birthday!" How could you not celebrate your birthday? Trying to hide from us, is it? I was so embarrassed. I was not used to the attention and more than that I didn't believe I was worthy to be celebrated. I didn't know all of them, maybe just a couple of them. But I was warmly hugged and genuinely wished on my birthday. I felt so special and loved. I was offered a drink by one of them. But Mia jumped to my defence and said, "Don't take that". And in her language (Portuguese) she chastised him. So, he left me alone. She led me to the other end of the coach to her room. It was all decorated with balloons, streamers and there was loads of food – meat of all kinds, dinner rolls, salads, chips. Enough to feed an army! "It must have cost a bomb", I thought to myself. I would later learn that an impromptu party just happened. Everyone pooled in and bought stuff. Remember, there were some who did not even know me well. I made a plate and sat down to eat something. I wasn't hungry as I had had my dinner. Suddenly, there was a huge cheering outside the door and the Happy Birthday song started. "What now?" I thought to myself in excitement. It was headed by the pie-car manager and a lovely birthday cake with candles and all. I was also handed a birthday card signed by all those who were present. Mia was with me and a few other girls joined in. The guests slowly seemed to peter out by midnight. And Cinderella had to return home to her room.

What a wonderful end to an almost non-existent birthday! This is a birthday that will stay with me forever. It was definitely a grand finale to the day.

Thus, slowly, I began to lose my fear of strangers in the circus world. I began to see how this unit of 300 people was a beautiful world to be in. They were just normal people living a life known to them. If anything, I was the abnormal one. We all looked after each other and everyone knew everyone's business. That was the norm.

CHAPTER 22

Living and working in that environment were unique because the thin line that separates the two often merges. Some days we don't know when the day's shift ends or when it begins – like on this typical working day. My school ended that day. It had been a challenging day and I was waiting to get to the comforts of my 7 × 12. The company vehicle was waiting at the assigned spot. This was the mini-van. The driver was my Colombian friend Cynthia. She and I were close in age, and I liked her ever-cheerful personality. So, we hung out together quite often. I always sat in front of the van with her. But I noticed someone was already seated there. I walked towards the van irritated. My friend was standing outside and finishing a smoke. She waved to me and signalled to creep to the other side of the van. I could do with some distraction, I thought. She had the best corporate gossips – not harmful, just sharing information with a giggle here and there. Without any hesitation, I hurried to where she stood all agog for what she was going to tell me. She always knew who was having an affair with whom, who was pregnant, who was cheating on whom, or who was being hired or fired. She always knew when there was going to be a visit from the higher-ups in the company (who didn't obviously live on the train). When I got close to her, in a very animated whisper, she said Dave the GM was going to get fired. Dave was a good guy. I was shocked and sad. I asked, "Why???" And just as she was about to tell me, I noticed the man in the passenger seat slumping. Initially, I thought he was bending to pick something up from under the seat. Then I asked my friend, "What is he doing?" She looked and then screamed, "Get into the van NOW, Manna". I got in and called to the man who was leaning forward. No response!

My friend drove like a maniac – weaving through traffic. I tried to pull him up from the back seat but he was too heavy. Suddenly she said, "Call Dave and tell him Jerry is having a heart attack and we are taking him to the hospital". "Heart attack?" I asked in a squeaky voice. "Call Dave, Manna", she yelled at me.

I did it in a trance, all the time wondering how the US would deal with two ladies (both non-Americans) arriving to the hospital with a dead body. And how did she know he was having a heart attack? Wasn't she a heavy vehicle driver? Shouldn't we have told someone at the Arena first, before racing off with a dying man? All of these thoughts had no answers or perhaps would never be answered. We were on a mission, to save a man's life. I called Dave who would have thought that I was either drunk or completely over-reacting to something very simple. Finally, he just asked me one question, "Which hospital are you heading to?" I asked Cynthia to which she barked out an answer. I felt inept.

Anyway, we reached and she parked right in front of the emergency and in her thick accent started shouting, "Help! Heart attack" No one could understand her. People were trying to calm her down, perhaps thinking that she was having a heart attack. I walked up to the nurse at the reception and told her about our unconscious colleague in the van. The nurse moved into action.

In seconds, Jerry was rolled in. In the meantime, Dave, the manager, and Steve, the payroll guy (he deals with insurance), arrived. A long wait ... the doctors came out and said, "He's going to be ok. They got him here on time". The Indian and the Columbian had just saved the life of the American!

During the wait, I sat alone avoiding eye contact with Dave as I knew he was going to be fired. I knew that he didn't know about it as yet. I didn't know Steve well so I didn't know what to talk to him. As for my friend Cynthia, she was busy talking to almost all the people standing around.

After the news from the doctor, we were told by the manager that we could leave. Cynthia had to shuttle people to and from the train. No time for theatrics. The show must go on, both in the ring and outside the ring. No one stops. Everything went on well and Jerry got back to work soon.

This made me think, "Do we fuss a lot with our patients?" So many unwilling people attending to patients in our hospitals. We blame it on "culture".

I was glad to be back in my room. It was too much after a rough school day. I was tired, scared, confused. Nothing seemed to faze Cynthia. She was chirpy, proud she had saved a life. I sat numbed with many unanswered questions.

Why was Dave being fired? He was a good man, kind and caring.

How did the bus driver know the man was having a heart attack? Will Jerry survive? If not, will we be blamed?

I realized Cynthia was talking nineteen to a dozen about people around the ER. Someone was shot, someone had an accident, someone had consumed poison ... I was partly listening to her but for the most part I was in my own world.

When she paused for taking a breath, I asked, "Cynthia, how did you know he was having a heart attack?"

She suddenly went quiet. Then said in a soft sad voice, "I used to be a registered nurse back in my country". She had had to take up the first job that came after her husband brought her to the US and abandoned her and the kids. She lost her vivacity and was thoughtful. I felt a sisterhood of having swam against a similar current and fought a fight that only mothers do for their children.

We reached the train (our home) in silence. As she was dropping me off, I said, "Come in for a coffee". She replied, "No honey, you look like you need a margarita". With a wink, a wave and a deceptive smile, she was gone – gone to continue with her duty of driving the bus with a nursing degree hidden somewhere in her room among other treasures. Some women make such sacrifices when saddled with dead beats as husbands.

CHAPTER 23

Believe me I'm grateful for the opportunities. But it's unfair if I keep you all thinking everything was a success story. So, here I am, sitting down to do a quick appraisal of my life in general: what making a leap meant; what leaving a seemingly good marriage meant; what worked and what didn't. How would I rate myself as a teacher, an influencer?

Was it all great? No.

Did I have failures? Yes.

Hence, to keep my feet on the ground and also to show you the bumpy journey, I thought I would do a quick evaluation of the struggles and pain at the personal and professional level. Therefore, these incidents are mostly about what didn't work.

First, at a personal level, my relationship with my mother was a mess. Initially, as a little girl, it was extremely confusing, I had no idea why she didn't like me. I know there have been a lot of reassurances from others that it was not true. But I am just going with my feeling for most part. Rejection.

Then came my first love. After believing for seven years that this was the person with whom I was going to be for the rest of my life, it didn't happen. This is not the place or time to get into the blame game. But this taught me I could continue to love the person, and "happily ever after" may sometimes just mean reliving the memories forever.

Then came the marriage, and what a twisted mind I had to think that marriage was a way to escape from the environment which was degrading me and stifling me gradually. Rather late, I realized that's the wrong reason to be married.

Then came children. I think I did pretty well. Asking grown up boys if I had been a good mother is never going to end well. Either they will lie, to avoid confrontation and drama, or they will tell me the truth and I may be mortified to know the truth. I love them. They love me. Period.

At a professional level, I have worn many hats and all of them looked pretty. Or most of them looked pretty. My job as a counsellor in Loyola was a job and therapy. The indirect lessons learnt were more than the direct ones: how to be organized, how to move past differences and biases, gaining technical skills as a counsellor, and so on.

I discovered a skill I never knew I had … that of training people. Although I became extremely confident about training people, I could never pursue that. My stint with adoption both in India and internationally opened my eyes to another realm that was emotional. Dealing with couples yearning for a child, while at the same time another couple considering terminating the pregnancy opened my eyes to a world full of contradictions. Later when I left India, I had no idea all these scattered experiences would come in handy. I never thought that all the people who come into my life would leave an imprint on me.

A high-school student at the Circus School was not interested in school. He was a dropout. And getting back to school was not by choice. He was coming to my class because he was part of a troupe at the show. Academics was the last thing on his mind. My thoughts were, "Now that he was in my class, I should teach him something".

All my hope of the Pygmalion effect didn't work. I gave my soul. I spent hours making his IEP. I tried taking him out for coffee. I tried to make him see that not everyone was rejecting him. I tried ... God knows I tried – not to just teach him to write his name, but to see his own value. I just wanted him to know he was a precious youngster. His life mattered. He was counted. But a year after he left, he got into his old world of gang fights and drugs. Someone shot him dead. The part of town he came from was not kind to him. They did not value him.

The next one was so nifty in stealing cars, or car parts. He was free from that the two years he was at school. But he went back to his old life when he left the school. He ended up in jail. Sometimes you just cannot have the Prof. Higgins effect, or as someone said, the "To Sir With Love" ending. All we can do is give our best. Some take it and bloom. Some just blow it all away. These were the two instances where I failed to make a mark as a teacher.

One learned to write his name and I took pride in calling him literate. The other stayed clean of larceny while at the show and had me fooled into thinking that he had changed. I didn't get the core of their being, did I? It was a failure.

A couple with four children gave up on their marriage. The woman caught the man cheating, literally with his pants down. Her eldest was of another man and this boy was in my class. He told me his parents were fighting, and his mother was going to take him and go away to their country. I hugged him and tried comforting him saying, "We adults can be worse than kids sometimes". I did not know the gravity of the situation. He looked at me with tear-filled eyes, held on to me tightly and said, "Ms. Manna I don't want to leave your school". "You are not going to leave my school", I said not knowing I was lying. It ripped my heart. I decided to intervene. I spoke to both the man and his wife. He was full of remorse and said he needed her forgiveness. She was not willing to give in. She was so angry, she could not see reason. I know, in her place, I too would have reacted similarly. They packed and left. The man wept like a baby. I stood helpless. I made the lady promise to stay in touch. The little first grader clung to me while saying goodbye.

The mother updates me about him. She put the child in a regular school in their country and he got on the honour roll of the principal. The mother thanked me for teaching him to learn. I am a good counsellor but here I failed.

In the middle of a school year, I had a kid brought to my class. Her father was on the unit. She had been living with her mother, who had remarried after the divorce. This little girl's world turned upside down when the mother met with a car accident and died. Now, the father had to take her back. The child seemed lost, extremely quiet and non-communicative. She was silently fighting her loss. The father was struggling to be a parent overnight. It was evident the father was finding it difficult to keep up with taking care of the child and his responsible position in the company. This is where the circus life proves to be different from the rest of the world.

Everyone is mindful of the other person. Therefore, we just jump in and do what is supposed to be done. So here I was, getting a kit ready with a tooth brush and paste, a hand towel and a comb. I, in fact, made one kit for each kindergarten kid. It came in handy for many little ones. It became part of my schedule to get her teeth brushed, feed her, comb her hair. No one noticed it. But the child loved me. I was her constant. Eventually, she also left the circus and went away to a regular school. But she is doing extremely well there. The father continued to be busy with work and being a father. But he remembered to send me a picture of the little girl with a certificate in highest proficiency. That's when I knew that although not acknowledged, he was aware of what I did for the kid. But I wish he had said, "You did well, Manna!" – at least once. Sometimes it is good to hear a word of appreciation, even when you know your worth.

An on-location educator of a circus adorns many hats – a mother, a nurse, a chef, a nanny, as the situation warrants. Since we all live together and work together, the switching roles is often too fast and inevitable. I had to preserve my individuality by keeping time for myself. I would call family and friends back in India and talk. Talking in a different language (Malayalam, Hindi and Tamil) and not having to talk about the circus was my saving grace. I didn't talk about the circus because some were embarrassed about me, while some didn't understand my job. Most thought I was living the life of a gypsy or a vagabond. But I wanted to know all about them, so I called and asked about all of them – the few minutes when I pathetically looked for love and validation!

Thinking about this part of my life is harder than I thought. I'll stop here. I'm not ready to relive those painful parts of my journey. I'll stick to the parts that make me seem strong, resilient and bold.

At one point in time, I had two cats with me on the train. That tiny little room became their home too. Initially, at 3 weeks, when they were in the confines of the train room, they were always in my way. I had to make sure that I didn't step on them when I moved around. They too finally made peace with the situation and decided to settle in. They hated when the train was being put together or put away. There were a lot of noises and slamming. I tried to stay with them on the bed, soothing them and calming them. It worked most of the time. I left them alone in the room when I was at school. They were fine as long as no one tried to enter the room. About others entering the room, we occasionally have room-safety inspections. We are informed ahead of time about this. Those with pets would have to inform the team to be careful about pets while opening the door. I always did it. However, my Moo (that was one and the other Piggy) hated men. Whenever I have tried telling this to the team, they laughed it off as a pet owner's exaggerated bragging. Pet owners are a lot like parents. They brag about their child at the first opportunity. Such was the attitude I got from some of them. Anyway, when the team entered, Piggy made herself scarce. She is the timid and shy one. Moo had seated herself on the top bunk and with a cool intimidating look, she kept looking at the person who had entered. Her look was scary. Her hair didn't stand on end, and she remained where she was. As the team member entered to look under the kitchen counter for the fire extinguisher, she just watched as all the others were passing comments on her. Moo understands every tone. She demands respect. When the guy straightened up after checking, he stood straight with his back to Moo. And like a lightning, in a blink, SWAT! His cap went flying. Thankfully he had the cap, or she would have clawed her way into his scalp. Everyone hurriedly left the room. There was no hissing, no hair-on-end, just one strong swat. If he was facing her, she would have gotten in his face. I don't even want to think about it. I got a message from the safety officer saying my room was not safe for others. I am not sure if it was a joke or he was annoyed that he was swatted like one would a fly. I wrote back with a smile, "Others shouldn't be in my room anyway". From then on, my room inspection happened when I was in the room. I would move both Piggy and Moo into the bathroom until the inspection of my room was complete. Moo was loving and affectionate. It was just that she didn't like men. Every evening, when I returned from school, Moo would be seated by the window, looking out for me. As soon as she spotted me, the look in her eyes changed, she would not move, but her eyes would soften. Moo had a personality which made me laugh. Piggy is the cute one. As soon as I entered the room, they needed a lot of attention – cuddles, cleaning of the litter box, and fresh food and water, in that order. Then they would curl up and sleep with loud snores. It is only after attending to them would I make my cup of coffee. Piggy and Moo have witnessed a lot of my tears and struggles. They were definitely my only comfort. The rough and tough Moo would allow me to hold her, only when she knows I am sad. Otherwise, she will decide when and how to get close to me. Piggy hated me crying. She couldn't handle it when I was not in control of my emotions. They lived with me for almost 13 years. They returned to India with me. What an adventure that was!

Their journey back to India with me was eventful. It took a year to line up the papers for them to travel. Their immigration into India was ten times more difficult than mine to the US. A vaccine showing they were fit to travel was to reach the Animal Husbandry Department in India. They had to then seal it and send an NOC (No Objection Certificate) back. All this had to happen in 10 days, because that's how long the validity of the vaccine was. When have we achieved any paper work in India in such a short time???? This kept going for a whole year.

Finally, I paid someone to physically go to the said place, get the seal and courier the document back to the US. It cost almost 25K. Yes! Why??? Well, my other option was to leave them behind. After 13 years, leave them behind? It wasn't going to happen.

They had to be put in pet carriers which were according to the specifications of Lufthansa. The pet carrier had to be lined with padding to absorb urine; food and water and extra food had to be arranged for them during transit in Frankfurt. It broke my heart to leave them there at the airport. They were micro chipped, vaccinated, all set. I remember walking into the Logan International Airport with two hollering cats and getting a lot of unsolicited attention. It's like a parent walking around with a child who was having a meltdown. I was also afraid that they may ask me to take the cats out of the cages so they can do a security scan of the cages. Just as I feared, I was asked to get them out of the cages, one at a time. You know my Moo. She hated men; she is vicious and aggressive. I was beyond stressed. However, the officer was so gentle with Moo; she was calm and allowed him to remove her from the cage without a fight. All cleared, and they were rolled away to be boarded on the plane. It broke my heart ... the look they gave me as they were taken away from me. I had a lot of questions about their safety and comfort. Will they be in a temperature-controlled place? Will someone check on them? Who feeds them? What happens if they are forgotten to be boarded on to the connecting flight? The officer patiently answered all my questions to my satisfaction and reluctantly I walked away to finish my boarding formalities and head towards the gate.

When we reached Frankfurt, and were disembarking, I kept looking out on the huge tarmac wondering if my babies could be spotted. Were they freezing? What if I found them dead in the cages? I had to distract myself from all the fearful and negative thoughts. I thought of my sons and their families. I thought of the preparation they would be making to receive me. It made me smile.

I resigned to the fact that I was not going to be allowed to carry the cats with me in the cabin anyway. It is what it is and the airlines seemed to know what they were doing.

When I landed in Chennai, I first ran to the customs, even before I went to the baggage claim. There was no sign of them. I could feel panic rising within me. On one side, my baggage making rounds on the conveyor belt, and on the other my sons waiting for me outside. Between these two, my fur babies were somewhere! Whom do I ask? What if they were still stranded in the US or were still in Frankfurt? I was filled with panic, hands sweating, heart beating like it was in my throat. And then I saw a young man push a trolley. He had the cages stacked one on top of the other, and the whole thing was covered with a sheet. I ran towards it. He was pushing it towards the customs officer. I ran and asked permission to just see them. The officer ignored me at first, and he lifted the sheet and said in a dismissive tone to his colleague, "They are just cats". What was he expecting? Crocodiles? No one calls my cats "just cats"! They are NOT "Just Cats". I kept my cool and demurely approached the just-cats-officer. "Please, may I just see them? They have been away from me for the last 27 hours". He looked at me quizzically. Few people in India understand the love humans have for their pets. For most, they are "just cats". It may have been providential, or probably the tear-filled eyes moved him. He nodded and waved his hand as though to say, "Go ahead". I ran to the trolley and lifted the end of the sheet that covered them and all hell broke loose. Both Piggy and Moo started literally complaining, cussing in unison, as soon as they saw me and heard my voice. I wanted to hold them so badly. I had tears rolling down my face, apologizing. I had abandoned my own boys for over a decade. All of that remorse came over me. I wiped my tears and lifted my head to see half a dozen customs officers standing around us and watching amusedly at the emotional reunion. I handed over the file with all the documents for the "just cats" to enter India. The officer did not even take it from me. He waved his hands and said with a friendly smile, "Go home and take these noisy cats with you". I pushed the cart as quickly as possible as many amused people were watching, and almost walked out when I remembered my baggage was probably on some carousel making rounds. I hailed a helper staff and asked him to help with my suitcases and then walked out to my home soil, Madras, sons and all things good. In the car, Piggy and Moo occasionally complained, especially when my sons and I got a bit loud with our excited conversations. My son who had spent a crazy amount of time getting the documentation in order for Piggy and Moo in the last one year expressed his disapproval at the customs officer not even looking at the documents. He said, "Technically, they have not entered India!!!"

We reached the place where I was planning to stay for a few days until Piggy and Moo got settled, a room to myself. I had asked for a litter box and some wet cat food. It was ready. As soon as they were let out of the cage, both ran to the litter box. Moo had to wait in line for her turn. Poor things, they had not wet the padding in the cage and now were relieving their bladder. My sons and I stood in reverent silence and allowed them their privacy. But we were giggling all the time. It was a sight I couldn't ever erase from my mind. Since then, Piggy and Moo have moved four houses. Each time, they adapted easily and slowly became Madras girls, just like me.

CHAPTER 25

Two years after being in the US, things had changed. From being in cold damp places with no proper warm clothes or winter shoes, I now found myself in a different winter land while I was with The Greatest Show. I had a room well heated, I had food and I had friends. I had a job where I was loved and respected. The snow or the freezing cold could not touch my body or soul. I don't remember the show ever being called off because of the onslaught of snow. The tour for the year was planned in such a way that, under normal circumstances, there would be no snow days. But, yes, we have passed through some really cold terrains. Now the snow looked beautiful when looking out the window of my train home. Also, by now, I had blankets, boots, woollens and shoes. I was well-equipped for the winter. During these cold days, I noticed that the discussion on the train among the train crew was about keeping the pipes from freezing, and being ready and equipped for any emergency during the run. One of the main things the Train Master was concerned about was keeping the animal cars warm. The animal cars (coaches) had heaters. The water tanks and pipes were constantly checked to make sure they are not frozen. With my limited knowledge, I often wondered to myself what the fuss was all about. Until one particular year, when we were on the East coast in the middle of winter, this happened ... The entire train froze up. No water for anyone … man nor animals. I will never forget the train crew who were working 24/7 with blow torches to thaw and melt the pipes, to supply the animal cars with water for the elephants, horses, zebras and the llamas. Many of them crawled under the train to do their work. It was an emergency situation. The law of the land has specific rules and regulations for circus animals. Their safety and their well-being took precedence over everything else. My winters were better when I was with the circus. This probably is because there was a warm room to come to where I had access to filter coffee and a warm peppery soup. I had friends, I had jackets, sweaters, woollen socks and scarves. I didn't need to wrap my head and feet in scarves or shirts. I enjoyed my winters. The beauty of the snow-clad trees, the pure white blanket spread on the ground fit for a queen, an occasional scampering of a squirrel: all scenes that slide past my window as I sit in the comforts of my warm room. That's an experience money cannot buy. During these runs, some food tasted better than others. It is during these runs I realized that what we call "comfort food" also changes from time to time. Watching the snow and the cold, I loved sipping hot chicken soup, broccoli and cheddar soup, and, every once in a while, our Indian version of the lentil soup. Hot spicy chicken wings, every Indian's favourite, and briyani were the dishes I was craving for.

In all my years that I lived on the train, there was never a time I felt either insecure or scared. I never felt threatened either – perhaps a little during the first week and the first few train runs. Then it had become my home, my haven.

Living on the circus taught me the following:

Diversity doesn't have to be difficult; you don't have to pick your friends from a certain class; you don't have to speak the same language; you don't have to follow the same rules every day.

As much as people in every city loved the show, in some cities you get more love than others. In other cities, you could get a shower of stones as you are pulling into the city, or have the coaches vandalized while in the city. Why people did it I have no idea. If it was because of their love for animals, then what they did only bothered the animals. Anyways, all this and more made life outside the ring more real and exciting.

It was always difficult for my own people both in the US and back in India to comprehend why someone would want to live as I did – crammed up in a tiny space, with 299 others from all walks of life, some who have stories that are never told and some whose stories are repeated over and over. Aside from the fact that I had no choice, my answer in my head would be, "What's wrong?" But I always ended up saying, "I like it this way".

Let me stop and give it a thought here. How is it that these changes never seemed to drag me down? What kind of conditioning had I been trained in that I could adapt and blend in no matter how severe the change? Part of it is definitely the moves and changes I have had to endure as a child because of my dad's job. Part of it definitely is the attitude of my parents who made it all seem like, "Hey! We are on to another adventure!" That's how I saw my changes. Hey! Here comes another adventure.

One of the scariest things about the circus life was the encounter with death. While everything goes on smooth and follows a routine, it is fine. But life throws in a wrench when you least expect it.

It was a day like any other
Same cares, same stress, same bother
Little did I know, lurking in the day
Was the tryst with death, if I may say
I went about my work, as I always did
When out of nowhere a tingling slid
From my head to my arms neck and feet
I took a sip of water, got up from my seat

In a flash I saw my children in my mind
I rushed to my colleague, she who was kind
Need a paramedic, something was not right
She moved into action seeing my plight
Rest was a blare
The ambulance
The paramedics
The words floating around
Trauma Centre
She's going in for a stroke
I whispered his name and handed my cell
To the paramedic who sat by my side
All went silent as he held my hand
You will be fine ma'am I'll make sure you are
As we pulled into the hospital
I looked into the eyes of the paramedic
"He isn't coming, is he?" I asked
"No ma'am. He said he's busy right now"
Alone in a strange place
Alone in that cold place
Alone I lay in a daze
Alone with tears on my face.

As the gurney was rolled in, the paramedic still holding my hand reassured me that the blood pressure had come down. "You will be fine ma'am", he said cheerfully. I looked at him to see if he was trying to convince himself. Soon I was surrounded by doctors and nurses and one of them said, "We've got this". The paramedic slowly let go of my hand. As I was rolled away, he stood there smiling. The kindest smile I had seen in a while. Were there tears in his eyes or were they mine?

In a few minutes and a few jabs later, I thought to myself, "Where am I?" Reality began to return. I started feeling calmer. How would I get back to my 7×12? I had no clue and didn't think anyone would come from the place of work to pick me up, as it was time for the show to start.

The show always goes on. I'd been in this city for just 3 days. I had no clue how to go about. I felt a slight pang of anxiety and said a prayer. That's when suddenly a face came to my mind. She used to come home when she was 12. She was all grown up and lived in that very city. She had called me a few weeks back to catch up. "I'll see you in Dallas when you get here", she had said as she ended the conversation.

I scrolled through my phone and found her number and asked the nurse who was close to my bed to make a call. I wasn't even sure what kind of a response I would get. The phone rang and was presently connected to the one person I knew in that town. Was she working? Would she get time off? And if she cannot come, then what will I do next? As these questions raced through my mind, the nurse handed the phone back to me with a smile and said, "She is coming".

I closed my eyes and let that sink in. "Someone is coming for me". In under an hour, the young lady stood before me scrubs and all. No more the 12-year-old, but a woman with a purpose, calm, composed and smiling. She first checked with me if I was feeling ok, and then as soon as she heard about my state, she talked to the nurses and the doctors. I watched her conduct herself … so adult so grown up.

Right then, the doctor came around and passed his verdict, "Pressure stabilized, go home and rest". I did not even show the courtesy of thanking the doctor Instead, I turned to the young lady who was standing by my bedside and pleaded, "Please drop me at my 7 × 12". She retorted in a tone that left no room for argument, "Oh no!" She was fully in charge now, "I'm taking you home for some love and rest; your circus can run without you for a bit".

The doctor had prescribed three days of rest. Not sure if my little friend had convinced him to do that. But it was a much-needed break. Either way, those 3 days I slept and slept, and allowed her to pamper and nurse me to be fit and well. I was feeling at my best. As I packed to leave on the third day, rested and calm and loved and blessed, I felt tears stinging my eyes. Gratitude.

Suddenly she said from the doorway, "You bought me my first bra, do you remember?" she said. My tear-brimmed eyes matched hers.

Soon I was in the train yard and dropped off by my home-on-wheels. A quick hug and a smile was all we exchanged as she headed out to her job, and I to mine. The whole incident taught me lessons which I have heard my parents repeat but never understood. First, help always comes from unexpected places. Second, the people you think are the ones to look after you are never the ones who do. Third, there is a Force, always and I mean ALWAYS, that has looked out for me.

A Force that can pull me out of the gates of death and destruction.

Some give it no name. Some call it the Almighty; some say God. I say, my Lord and my God.

CHAPTER 26

It was so good to get back to work after 3 days – new found energy and new appreciation for every child in the class. The class had many posters and banners saying "Welcome Back, Ms. Manna". There were also many lessons to catch up. After the initial hugs and expressions of love, we slowly settled down on classroom mode. Soon there was silence and each child was busy at work. I loved it when the class was absolutely disciplined. These kids are so resilient and adaptable that it is hard to explain. We advocate stability for children and their growth, especially during their formative years. I used to be a strong advocate of that myself.

However, being at the circus and watching the life of children from birth to adulthood has made me rethink. I found the circus kids more adaptive, more hands-on and more cheerful. This is something to really ponder over.

Parental expectations are low here. I think I need to rephrase that. Parental expectations are realistic. Parents do not have a mindset where they think their child needs to be the topper at all times. The attitude of entitlement is not there in the children. They see and behave like all are equal. Every once in a while, there is conflict that crops up when we have a new person join the circus. They need time to fit in and get used to the environment.

Understanding field trips and planning for them was more difficult than actually preparing 60 odd plans for a day. I have to admit, it took me a good 6 months to realize that the field trips could be a huge part of learning. With all my lesson planning, I now had to incorporate field trips into the plan. Their regular subjects could be clubbed with places of interest in every town. All I needed was some extra planning. I knew it meant more work for me. I am not one to shirk responsibility or work, and I am one who loves to take up challenges. Thus, I started looking at our annual roster for the tour of cities. I would then plan a field trip and integrate the science, math, history lessons into places of interest and/or importance. Things began to gain momentum; children began to discover a new-found interest in their lessons. I was over-loaded but loving it.

On one occasion, we were in San Antonio, Texas. On browsing Google, I found Alamo was steeped in history and I remembered one of the grades was reading that as their lesson. I sat down to get the stats of this place, the history, the battle, the transition from it being a mission to a battle field. The possibilities of the knowledge the children (mind you all grades) would gather was phenomenal. I made worksheets, I gave a brief idea of what to look for, I made teams comprising bigger and smaller students and we were good to go. And when they returned, the next day would be spent in putting together all the information they had gathered and making a presentation for the class and sometimes the parents. The learning that takes place during such trips and the teamwork is beyond belief. Even the little elementary school kids would be rattling off details of the Alamo. I may not have followed the curriculum to a T but I really saw knowledge find its way into the minds of the kids. There was fun, there was work and there was knowledge. What more can we ask for? My students started getting eager to be in school and were looking forward to being in class. I did not have to drag them into the class or their lessons. They started looking up cities ahead and bringing in ideas of places we could visit. I am very proud of what I have achieved and know the kind of education those kids got was par excellence. This is the reward for every teacher – to see the students yearning for school time. Never before or never after have I had such a fulfilling experience in teaching. It's a nugget I cherish and hold close to my heart. Education is more than merely answering questions, it is more than learning to spell, add and subtract. Education is when you know how to answer a question; it is when you know how to make a correct decision or when you can think beyond biases and prejudices.

Of all the activities or rather moments of learning we have had in the class, the top of the list would be the field trips, closely followed by compiling all that they saw and understood into a project not just for themselves but also for the entire unit. The folks at the unit were always agog with the eagerness of little kids to see what next the school came up with.

Now, before I seem like some flawless superwoman, I will let you in on a secret. I made teaching fun for me. I needed to enjoy what I was doing, before I got the students involved. My idea of education has never been about feeding a few formulae or definitions into their tiny brains. It was more about making them good human beings. Respect, Appreciation, Gratitude (RAG) had to become a way of life while learning the 3 R's. That was the Heart of the Circus.

Thus, I decided to make us (my students and me) well integrated into the circus. One which stood out was a field trip that was done right there, on the location where we were. Charity begins at home, doesn't it?

Most of us knew the performers, management and maybe even the concessions. But there were many other departments that worked like well-oiled wheels to make this 12-month-long tour seem easy: the train crew consisting of the train master and his crew, transportation department, wardrobe, production, purchasing, light and sound, the band, the animal crew. I, therefore, thought going through each department and learning their job descriptions and responsibilities would enable us to have a better appreciation of what they did at the circus.

The train had a train master and the train crew: about 10 to 12 people. They took care of the maintenance and cleanliness, and made sure all had a pleasant stay. Since they were at the train and did not come to the Arena, they went unnoticed.

That's how I decided to undertake a project where my students would visit the train and spend a whole day with the crew to learn about their work and the working of the train. This was a huge success. For the first time ever, the train crew felt counted. The students were divided into groups and sent with each crew member to learn about wiring, watering, electrical, plumbing, septic cleaning, and so on. By the end of the day, they knew a lot more than most managers. They heard about things like changing wheels on a train, garbage disposal, generator car and its maintenance and so on. And we are talking about Grades 1 to 12. Everyone got something out of it.

The next day was spent in making presentations and getting ready to exhibit what they learned to the other circus folks. I learned that although there were kids who couldn't write their names on a straight line, they had an aptitude and interest in the mechanics of the train. I ended up questioning myself about what education really is. Should we feed children with a whole lot of info which we barely use on a daily basis or should we instead feed them information they are ready to receive and put into use?

It was a learning experience for all including those who had never had an opportunity to go to school. In a way, if you think about it, I was probably a teacher for the whole unit … not just for the kids under 18, although there was no such intention when I was hired for the job that cold winter month in Detroit.

You ask my students why the Statue of Liberty is green in colour, or who built it, or what one would find on the Ellis Island. All of my students from Grade 1 to the high-schoolers will give you facts and figures, appropriate to their age.

If you are thinking that their knowledge and learning was limited to the US alone, you are mistaken. One of the biggest and most enjoyable learning experiences for both the teacher and students happened when we planned on an event called In Foo Fe (International Food Festival). For a city that moves on wheels and is in a new town every week, this was not going to be easy. Yet we pulled it off. We started with what resources we had on hand. For us, it was people from about 27 different nationalities – Morocco to China, Russia to Argentina, covering most latitudes and longitudes we had at the show. That's when I realized there may be a lot of them missing their homeland and families. It was strange that I found that comforting.

I divided the class into groups with the senior students being leaders and the others being reporters. We planned a questionnaire and all the people were interviewed by my students, in some cases with interpreters. We asked about their clothes, their homes, their food and their schools. We then looked up their position on the map, the size of the country they come from and their flags. All the students had to learn the flags of these 27 countries at least. Flags and capitals of the countries became knowledge at their fingertips. We made charts, display models and the finale was when we asked each of these different nationalities to bring the dish that was typical of their country. By this time, this food festival that the circus school was organizing became the talk of the "town". We even had to look ahead and coordinate with the train master to find a train yard that would be conducive to this food festival where all the people could gather and share the food. The whole unit pitched in. The train master and his crew helped with the set up of laying tables out for all the food. Beside each food stood the flag of that country, waving proudly. India had her Briyani out there for all to taste. The take away from this event was my students learned team work; they learned different things about people they had never talked to before. Not only did the students (including me) learn a lot, we brought the unit together under one umbrella through food – what better place than around a dining table for a magic to happen.

CHAPTER 27

Life was not all school. Life at the circus was a miniature stage acting out everything that was happening in the world outside of it. After all, these were humans like those outside the tent. We had births and deaths, relationships, breakups, weddings, job losses, ill health, fights. The only thing if I may say was different from life outside of us was that everyone irrespective of age and position were in one way or the other involved in it all. What the world would consider "being in others'" business was really the way of life at the circus. Hence, baby showers were attended by all. A birthday meant time for celebration for all; new relationships meant there was rejoicing all around except a few regrets by some for having missed the boat. Nevertheless, everyone knew everyone's business. In the world outside, most of these things would have been considered as rude and impolite and even nosy. But no, not at the circus. If you don't get in another's business, it was considered rude and insensitive. This was not too much of a problem for me, as I came from a culture where everybody else runs your life for you, and everyone has an opinion on your life. So, in a way, I took it in my stride.

There were things that directly affected me. That would be when the birth, death, job losses, divorces, or illnesses directly affected my students. Those days were tough. The priority then becomes that particular child who is going through the trauma of a loss or confused at the shift in the family with the arrival of a newborn or the separation of the parents. Either way, the role of a teacher is accentuated. I realized that I was the only constant in the child's life. To stay strong enough to walk the child through, it was important.

After a few weeks into my circus life, I was very surprised to see a gentleman dressed in a robe and vestment walking back stage. He was a reverend father. If you were surprised that a teacher ran a school at the circus, then this was a surprise for me. I was amused as I thought he had come to see the circus and was getting a tour of the back stage. I later found out that he along with two sisters (nuns) were part of a circus ministry. Interesting concept. The next few days my thoughts were around that. I realized that everything was well thought out. The spiritual needs of at least some people at the circus had to be taken care of. The priest and the nuns were there to offer pastoral guidance and care. A mass is usually planned around their visit. There would also be baptisms, confirmations and confessions, and counselling.

At one point, two of the sisters took up a job with the circus, thus being available 24/7 on the unit. It was comforting to know that there was a place to go for respite. They were there to make sure counselling, confessions, sacraments and any other ritual that pertained to the spiritual well-being of the people on the unit were taken care of.

I have never been a religious person. I am more spiritual than religious. To me rituals hold no meaning. But spiritual companionship was certainly missing from my life. Even as I carried on my duties, there was emptiness inside me. I was hoping I would meet a like-minded person at some point – someone who saw the One Almighty as I did – without the stuffiness, or the judgements. I may have prayed, or this deep desire of mine reached the right source. One day, I was walking down the hallway of the Arena, and people around were carrying on with their jobs. There was someone mending a float, another tinkering with the rigging, another driving the lions and tigers on to the ring for the morning practice. I was weaving my way through them all as though to get to work and meeting big cats was the most natural thing in the world. There in an insignificant corner sat a girl fixing the button on the dress of a star performer. She was one of the seamstresses. I would later find out she headed the department. I was not particularly curious or excited because sewing and me were poles apart. I wouldn't know what to do with a seam that's come off of my dress, or how to fix a button that had fallen off. I have used pins and even a stapler to get the seam back in place. Just as I passed her, I noticed something on her table. It just sat there and now I was staring at it. It was the Holy Bible. I then asked the stupid question, "Is that a Bible?" She looked at me rather annoyed and said, "Yes". Her tone held a few unsaid words like "What else does it look like?" I blurted out the next insane question, "So do you read it every day?" Before she could say anything, I said, "I would like to do it too". With that a whiff of a smile appeared on her face. I said, "I'm the teacher, Manna". She told me her name, we exchanged numbers and I ran to my class. That was the beginning of a deep friendship that is to this day. We initially had Bible-reading sessions, but later it turned to just sharing the week's news session. We usually met on days when we were loading out of a town. Both of us would pack our stuff into our respective boxes and would head out to our rooms. I finished as early as 3 pm. She couldn't till the last show was over. So she used to come to the room by about 10 pm. She loved our Poori & Aloo (it's a kind of bread deep-fried and eaten with spiced mashed potatoes). She loved butter chicken and parotta and briyani … We would share some really atrocious stories of the week's events. We would laugh till we cried and it would almost be 4 am before she retired to her room.

How do I describe her? Caring? Compassionate? Loving? Honest? A true friend? She was, perhaps, all of the above. She was as old as my children so I guess she was a daughter that I never had. She cared for me as a daughter would, but laughed with me as a BFF would. Maybe we didn't do much of Bible Reading or prayer, but she certainly was another angel in my life.

We have not seen each other but she left with me something for a lifetime. She presented me with a pair of scissors. She told me to snip up old clothes and sew them back together. With the help of an old sewing machine, I sewed quilted hand cloths for my kitchen. I even made aprons of different styles by spending two dollars to get some fabric and made 4th of July–themed apron's for dad, mom and two kids and sold it as a set and made $100! Teach a man to fish and he will never go hungry!!!!

CHAPTER 28

It was year 2012, and I was getting ready to return to India. Piggy and Moo and the formalities of bringing them delayed the process. By then I had written my first book. *Bent, Yet Unbroken*. Started in 1998 and after each edition, it turned from a book spewing anger and bitterness into a much abstemious one. Call it cathartic if you will. My first grandson was born the same year and my children wanted me to come down for the baptism. This would be a short visit after the earlier emotional one. I decided to find a printer somewhere and get it printed and published.

I would talk about it in my school room and the whole school was excited for me, publishing my first book. My sons and their wives back home had it all planned and organized because I had less than 10 days for the book launch and the baptism. The book was printed and when I got to India, I not only held my first grandson but also held my book in my hands. The launch which was arranged in Marriot, Chennai, was an amazing experience – recognition, achievement, healing all rolled into one. The children showing their appreciation and love for me, and to be at the receiving end of love and care was an unforgettable experience.

I returned to the US with a few books for my close friends. My students were agog with anticipation to see the pictures and hear the story. I was like a little kid opening presents on Christmas morning. I narrated with great aplomb the whole story of my first book release. There were a lot of Oohs and Ahhs. I noticed one kid, Matthew, a second grader, sitting with a deep and serious look. I asked him, "Aren't you happy for me, Matthew?" He said, "I want to write a book too". That moment of pride for a teacher when a student says he wants to emulate you … it's priceless. It was a moment when I realized every minute I had spent with these children was well worth it. I walked up to him and with equal seriousness said, "You can. Write a story about anything and bring it to me and I will do a book launch for you here at the circus". To all teachers out there, don't let a moment to inspire someone go to waste. At least give it a try. He said a very unemotional, "OK". But that's Matthew, he gets quiet when he has serious things on his mind. The week was over, and to be honest, I forgot about it. When we reached the next city and the first day of school, Matthew walked in with a few sheets of paper and handed them over to me and said, "I wrote this book". My jaw hit the floor. The book was titled *Rudy*. It was a short story about a dog. The front cover had the picture of a dog. It also had the following words: Written and Illustrated by Matthew Iverson. The inside cover had these words: Dedicated to my teacher, Ms. Manna. I could only hug this second grader. The first ever book dedicated to me. I put aside everything planned for that day and gathered all the students around and we started planning for the launch. We printed out copies, tied them together, sent invitations to parents and others on the unit, and decorated the school room. I had one of the seniors called as a Chief Guest, another to be the MC, and had one of Matthew's classmates escort him in. The parents and the others came, and they all stood in line to get his autograph. It was, indeed, a moment of great pride for me. I hope one day soon this teenager would write a book and have it published and will invite me to witness it.

Such a fulfilling and satisfying life I had. Unique in every sense.

CHAPTER 29

Just when I had made up my mind to return to India and mentally told myself that I was going to lead a peaceful quiet life, there was an announcement. We were making a detour from the regular tour and were going to Mexico. I couldn't believe my ears. I had always wanted to go to Mexico, especially when I was touring California. Somehow it never happened. Suddenly I realized that Piggy and Moo were going to be with me. What would I do with them? Who would take care of them? My heart dropped and I thought perhaps I should return to India before the trip to Mexico came up. It never occurred to me that we could be going by train. I never thought of asking anyone either. After a few hours of panic, I got a mail giving information about the border-crossing in Laredo. I was ecstatic. So here I was going to enter one more country, before I returned to India.

I heard the train ride to Mexico took 7 days. I dreaded it. 7 days on a train?? Would I get cabin fever? I'm going to have issues with connectivity that was for sure. How would I survive not hearing from or talking to my family and friends? Will Piggy and Moo get sick? All the "what ifs" and "supposes" came up to haunt me. They took away the excitement of going into another country. There was nothing I could do about it.

Life throws you surprises. The long time on the train turned out to be something I needed.

We had started out from Columbus, Ohio. We wound our way south through Alabama, Louisiana, Texas, and with immigration formalities at the border in Laredo, we rolled into Mexico. However, before I get caught in the sombreros and tacos and tortillas ... and my personal jaunt to the Indian Bazaar in Mexico, a little peep into what the long run did for me.

I had:

Time for introspection.

Time to see the larger picture of what my place was in the universe.

Time to catch up with friends on the train. People walked in and out of my room for filter coffee and Indian food.

Time to cook with no distractions.

Time to read.

Time to pray.

Time to read more.

Time to write.

Time to make new friends.

Time to listen to music.

Time to sing along with my favourite songs of Praise and Worship and Country love songs.

Time to say "Hello self".

Above all, I had time to feel the lightness in my soul that was absent for a long, long time.

And to think I dreaded this long 7-day run!!!!

Crossing the border, and getting into Mexico, was exciting. Everyone on the train was out on the vestibule catching the first glimpse of Mexico. What did I expect? Anyways, what I saw was some run-down buildings with graffiti on the walls. It reminded me of the commute on our local trains back in Chennai. Don't ask me why or what's the likeness. It just reminded me of home.

Soon we stopped for a refill of food for both animals and humans. That was a long stop. Also, the septic tank cleaning, refilling of water and then we would be heading off to Mexico City, our home for the next one month. Piggy and Moo found their perch by the window. They were not going to miss any of the scenic beauty of Mexico.

The 4-day run to the border was rejuvenating, peaceful and filled with "me" time. I had forgotten what it was to relax and not worry about lesson plans and school. But now it was just my Piggy, Moo and me. Not all my students could travel to Mexico. Most had either problems with their passports or visa. So that left me with just one student.

Then late at night on the fourth day, I got a text

message which dropped my heart into a pit. I was told that the cats needed a health certificate to cross over to Mexico. Although I refer to them as cats, they are my babies. I adopted them when they were 3 weeks old. They have been with me since. I fed them, loved them, pampered them. I talked to them in Malayalam, Tamil and English when I missed home. They listened. They hated my tears, but tolerated it uneasily, when it flowed down.

The train moving at 60 mph and my mind at 100 mph, I felt dizzy. I wanted to throw up. What did this mean? Did it mean if I did go to Mexico, I would have to abandon my babies in the US? Or did it mean that I get off the train with them at Laredo. The only thing I knew about Laredo was rather a dismal song about carrying a corpse down the streets of Laredo. And that is not a happy song at all. It is more of a dirge. Well, I knew one more thing. I knew that that's where our immigration formalities were to happen.

Here is a rhetorical question. If at the immigration you are told that your babies cannot travel with you, would you just drop off the babies at the nearest dumpster and walk on? ... I didn't think so. I would never do that. I wept that night as I watched both my babies on either side of my bed stretched out, oblivious of the fact that their fate was being decided by some creatures called "people".

From being happy and relaxed, I was now a bundle of nerves, planning to get out and into the streets of Laredo.

Next morning, all I got was a call before my babies were whisked away. No time to protest, no time to plan, no time for goodbyes. They were being taken to the Vet (stranger) by another stranger (our circus staff). I was told they will be brought back as soon as possible. So, with my babies hollering and crying in fear, they were taken away. Simultaneously we were asked to clear out of our rooms and go to a tent for immigration formalities. The temperature was racing to a scorching high, threatening to touch a 100°F. This was Texas and Summer. My heart was beating a rhythm that was, what I then thought, how it would be for the rest of my life. Or I thought it would suddenly stop because it couldn't take the pressure. An hour later I reached my empty room, devoid of my babies. The silence was eerie. It smelled of sadness. Now I have yet another stamp in my passport!! Exit US and ready to go into Mexico.

No news of my babies. I was a coward, I dared not call the concerned people to check. I was so afraid of the uncertainties.

In the meantime, I had to clean out my fridge and closet of anything that made me insecure. My mango pickle went out, followed by a new tub of yogurt, and milk for my coffee and eggs. I understood that certain food items were not allowed across the border. But to take away the very ingredients that gave me a feel of comfort? All I was left with were some sardines, marinated and spiced up to be fried. Fish was the only non-vegetarian food allowed.

I was NOT prepared for any of this. If I were an infant, I would have put a pacifier in my mouth, curled up and gone to sleep, or even sucked my thumb.

Almost 3 torturous hours later, I was informed my babies were back but I had to now resolve their immigration formalities.

Therefore, now I am back in the tent standing in line for the immigration formalities of Piggy and Moo. The babies are now hollering, sad, hoarse and panting because of the heat. One of the immigration officers asks me to take them out of the carrier. I try to explain that they will run away. I wanted to say they don't trust any of you. The Mexican authorities saw my tear-filled eyes and were sympathetic. They agreed to photograph the babies while in the carrier. There was this one lady who insisted they had to be taken out, and a voice in my head screams, "Why lady why? You want to be scratched and mauled?" Thanks to the sanity of the Mexican Immigration Officers! Formalities done and I was carrying my babies to the coolness of my room – back into their familiar place. They were back home. One runs to check the litter box. It is where it is. The other runs to the water and food. Everything was to their comfort. Then Piggy turns and looks at me accusingly, seeming to say, "What the heck was all that about?" and "Who were those humans, who did not talk to us but talked about us all the time?" I cried once more and through my tears said, "I am sorry baby". It was very reminiscent of the time I left my own children behind. "I did what was best for us", I said in a defeated tone. My heart whispered scornfully, "You Liar"!

The cats were now settled. I began to think of my 3-month stay in Mexico. I didn't know anyone there. Part of me was excited, the other part nervous. So much of biases of drug dealers and criminals. I had to protect myself. Therefore, before I left the US, I googled, "Indian community in Mexico". And all I got was the Indian Embassy. "That is so out of my league!" was my first thought. But then a little voice from inside prompted, "Here is a challenge, take it". For several days, I would scroll through that website and exit. Finally, one day, I opened my email and started,

Honourable Ambassador ...

I introduced myself as an Indian coming to Mexico with a circus. I asked for any Indian Association. The same day I got a response. A warm welcome and an invitation to dine with him, his family and other embassy staff. I was being invited by the Ambassador!!!!!

I could not believe it. All I expected was an email address of some Indian Association or the other, at best. Of course, I agreed. How often does that happen to an ordinary person like me?

The day came and a car picked me up and took me to lunch. There was the entire embassy, their families, and the Ambassador and his wife waiting agog to receive the Indian from the American circus.

I was served a sumptuous Indian meal and had to face a lot of questions – curious, enthralled, encouraging, appreciative.

The Ambassador was a friendly, witty, unassuming man. He kept the conversation going. Time flew past, and it was time for me to get back. But before that, I got invited to a couple of other homes of the embassy staff. I felt like a VIP. The frightened insecure Manna now felt at home in Mexico.

I got them all passes to the show. The Ambassador was seated in the VVIP seat. The management treated him with full protocol and respect. Although being the simple person that he is, it just amused him to see them run around making him comfortable. It definitely made me proud that the Ambassador and his wife accepted my invitation and that my circus management respected him.

CHAPTER 30

It is time I addressed the issue of "why?" How could you leave the two children behind? There was so much of drama unfolding back home and in my personal life. Each and every person who knew me directly or indirectly took sides. The ratio was unequal. A majority waited on casting the first stone. The ones who understood or sympathized with me were silenced. That's how the minority works. No matter how loudly the voice is raised, it is never allowed to be heard outside. They are suppressed inside a bubble, gaslighting at its peak! How quickly you fall from the pedestal when you stand up for something you believe in! How quickly friends and foes merge! How quickly the number of people around you dwindles to a zero!

I was left having to decide the next course of action. I could end it all or I could fight back and prove my point. But if fighting back against one person itself is daunting, fighting against a whole mob seemed impossible. It was a strange path I was on. No friends, no family. I could understand the family being offended as I turned into a solo swimmer; I was swimming against the tide while everyone else was drifting with it. This may have been difficult for them too in retrospect. I had believed all that they had been saying while I was growing up. I actually thought the liberal ideas and thoughts voiced in my home were meant for me too. It was only rather later that I realized that the rules and standards for me were completely different from what was laid out to the others. It was too late; I had already taken the leap. And now I found myself off the beaten path and on my own.

Disappointment, loneliness, rejection, along with estrangement from those I loved the most, unemployment, low funds, food running out, bitter cold winter, no sufficient warm clothes ... the beginning of the journey on the road less travelled. I had just begun and there was time to turn back if I wanted to. But there was also the adrenaline pumping urging me forward.

One way I dealt with this was by constantly looking at the bigger picture – by constantly making sure that I saw myself as a speck in the universe, instead of the centre around which the universe revolved. I also came to the realization that if I wanted value, I had to create value for those around me. It was about what I can do to make life easy for those around me. There would always be someone unhappy with my decisions, my thoughts, my actions, my looks. On the flip side, there would always be someone who would think I got it right. Thus, with that thought, I kept moving forward and waited for the world

I had left behind to see that we are just a speck and that's how it was always going to be.

The next best thing for me was to keep my eyes on the road I was on. Like a horse with the blinders, I trudged on. Nothing, and when I say nothing, I mean nothing distracted me. I kept on moving forward unsure yet determined, difficult, yet persevering. I had to for a bit leave my own children behind to fend for themselves. I threw a few scraps their way for their bare survival. This was the most painful part of my life. It would seem self-destructive to many. But sometimes you got to first put the oxygen mask over you first, before you put it on your children. I am to this day not sure if my children understood that, or if they felt abandoned in order for me to pursue my own dreams. That's what everyone does, right? When you say you are in the US of A, the immediate inference is "She is gone to live her dream". Except I had no dream. I had a desperate urge to stay alive. I had to stay alive as I had promised my son. This only God and I knew. The misconceptions and the prejudices of the people who believed in the fallacy that no woman can ever survive on her own, or a woman must be having a man behind her, wasn't making it any easier for me. Not only was it not making it easier, it was also hindering my progress. For every two steps forward, it was one step backward. Nevertheless, I never gave up. I knew me. I knew what I was worth. I knew that no one would know what I was worth. It slowly started being easier to let go of seeking validation from others and living with my conscience.

When I left India, I had left my eldest son behind, already in college. He seemed "Ok" when I said goodbye to him. But I am sure there would have been days, moments, when he would have wished I was around. He would have surely missed me. There may have been times when he wanted to return to the comforts of the home. Short breaks at college, long summer breaks, he just drifted from one place to another – from one relative's place to another, from one friend's place to another. I shudder to think, "Was he always welcome where he went?" "Did he invite himself?" I cannot undo the damage I had done. I cannot make amends ever for not being there for him. I have apologized several times. I have wanted to look him in the eye and say, "I am sorry for not being there". I haven't done it, neither do I think I can ever do it. I have said it on his birthdays, on New Year's and any other special moments. Not "said" per se, but written as an email or via messages. I do get guilt-ridden at times. I beat myself for being a horrible mother and thinking that parenting could be done remotely from miles across oceans. There is absolutely nothing I can do to undo that, is there? Lost time is really lost. Nothing will bring it back. I just learned to live around it.

I hear mothers rush to the sides of their children when they are in pain, sickness or in trouble. I have missed out on it. For instance, the time when the younger one was taken ill from hostel for an appendectomy – he did not lack love or care or support. But his mother was not there. I was in a place struggling for survival. The agony, the fear and the guilt kept eating into me. Or the time when my child passed out while driving and his pregnant wife was sitting on the passenger seat – right in the middle of the traffic. I read it in an email or was it over the phone? I did nothing. I could do nothing as I was miles away surviving.

I don't know what I have done right. I may have perhaps given them lessons in "what not to do". They are blessed and I am proud to see how they carry themselves about. I like to believe that somewhere, something was done right and I did have a part in it. I often wish I was one of those moms who kept their sons close to them all their life – pampering, babying and controlling. Some days I am filled with awe at the life of my children, and at other times, I feel so inept and incompetent.

My reflection one evening:

When I held you in my arms and prayed for wisdom beyond years,

I am not sure if I meant wiser than me ... but I am glad you grew wiser than me.

When I got your love and knew it was there to remain forever,

I didn't know I would have to share it with many others ...

Although I must say, I'm glad you are surrounded by love.

Every parent's prayer is their child is the most loved one ... life shows you otherwise.

When I prayed and taught you to live by your own terms,

Was I prepared for you taking wings and flying away?

Was I prepared for your rules? Or for you breaking mine?

I wanted you to lead while you followed me ... doesn't work that way, does it?

Wanted you to follow your heart but didn't realize your heart beat a different rhythm from mine!

Wanted you to look above the lines of religion but wanted you to have the Fear of the Lord.

Wanted you to love all, but I wished you would love some a little more than others ...

Wanted you to live a full life and wanted to give you the world ... but it never happened ... I failed over and over.

I wished you would have a pain-free life ... Wished I could remove all your pain ...

How could I when I have caused you pain myself?

Bottomline? Regret, sadness, and wistfulness are in a constant battle with pride, contentment and joy.

Time flew by and finally the 18-year-old left my side

to go into university and independence. When he went, I was left standing with desolation for company, fear as an accomplice and guilt as my bed-mate. That was the best I could do. I have often thought what my alternatives were. One was to keep him in Kuwait with me, while enrolling him in a distance education program for his graduation and getting him a driving job, or a super market bagging job. I would have had my son to support me and I could have got off the wagging tongues. My people couldn't fathom the independence and grit I had to carry on.

According to them, there always had to be a man. Actually, I am a man in a woman's body. By that I mean, I am capable of doing things which the patriarchal society assigns to men only – like running my own life and making my own decisions, and I am not saying this in a bragging tone. Go back and read the previous sentence in a matter-of-fact tone. I am bolder than most women and as bold and rough as most men. I wasn't born that way. I was born a soft, gentle, fun-loving, caring young girl. And as I traversed through life, I realized that "being nice" doesn't get me anywhere. I needed to get assertive. But assertiveness seemed to push people away from me. They were not used to that tone from me. At the same time, I found a whole new set of people who were welcoming the "new me". Subsequently, the panorama of my whole life changed and just like the snow melting and the first shoots of spring emerging, my life began to change. I accepted it wholeheartedly. Without much exertion, I could replace almost everything except my children. Once a mother, no replacement sits right. Even if I could, who would want to give up the two gems I had?

Bent, Yet Unbroken

The Second World War had hit Burma (now Myanmar) hard and my father was caught right in the middle of this holocaust ... I wonder what went through his mind at that time ... (My mind wandered as he kept narrating the gross details of the bombing and bloodshed). Was he thinking of the warmth and security of his home, a parsonage? Or was he being a masochist? Or was he punishing himself for the way he had caused grief to his parents in running away from home? Was he thinking of the hot broth served with lentils every night? Or was he thinking of the friends he had left behind? The dream of seeing his country free from the British rule was still vivid in his mind's eye. Free India ... The one thought that caused him to leave his home and be here in the midst of the shelling. Somewhere a choked voice caught my attention and I turned to see the moist eyes of my father. I had missed part of his narration while dipping into my own thoughts:

"Here was a chance to escape from there ... But here was also the conflict ... Should I use the ticket for the ship leaving to India with the refugees, to carry me or carry my sister, her new-born and her ailing husband?" *"I didn't have to think for long", said my father, "the fear*

and helplessness on the face of my sister standing there with her baby nuzzling to her warm breast and the helpless husband seated with a vacant stare was enough for me to decide". I told them to take the essentials and leave for the pier from where the ship was carrying passengers to Calcutta ... The ship sounded the horn and my sister, her baby and the husband bundled into an overcrowded ship, on their way to freedom and safety. I stood there on the pier as long as I could and then the deathly siren warning us to take shelter forced me to run for a trench. As I crouched in the trench, I let tears flow and fear and loneliness sweep over me, for I knew when I came out of that trench, I would have to make plans to get home.

I hadn't made many friends while I was staying in Burma. There were two others who I had grown to love and build up a brotherhood, the kind that seems to spontaneously grow between people in times of crises. The three of us sat down and made our plans, and we decided to walk towards the border. We never ever told each other our fears, instead kept talking about things we would do "WHEN" we got home, not "IF" we got home. We kept our sense of humour, our faith in God and our love for each other flowing consistently. We had to, because as we moved forward food was becoming scarce and water was becoming impossible to use. Trenches could no longer be used, as there was the stench of death everywhere. Mutilated human life strewn all over reminded us of the short span of our lives and the fallacy of man when he makes plans for the future. We trudged on stopping every once in a while to make a little fire and eat something to nourish us. We would rest at night under trees. The difficult part was when we had to walk through the jungles. We had little or no knowledge about the ways of the jungle. We did not know what crawled around or what lurked in the darkness of the night. We may as well have been three blind men walking. Days passed to weeks and we were beginning to feel the tiredness creep on us sooner than when we started out. One of my friends was showing signs of illness from an infected wound, and we had to slow down allowing him to rest. A couple of days later, he had a swollen foot and was burning hot. We rested under a tree and tried to cool his forehead with wet cloth. But he seemed to slip into oblivion. We sat there helpless just praying for a miracle. There were other people who were walking by and no one stopped for more than a couple of minutes and not many people had the energy to carry any more burden than they already had. Some stopped enough with words of comfort. Some looked imploringly with their eyes to forgive them; some offered a coat or an extra piece of cloth to keep him warm. The nights were spent under the tree waiting for death to lull him to eternal sleep. As we huddled and waited, my friend opened his eyes once and said that he would want us to move on. But we wouldn't hear of it. I reassured him that things would be ok and we would move when he got better. In exasperation or trust, I will never know which one, my friend closed his eyes and slipped into what seemed to be a peaceful slumber. We watched the steady breathing and somewhere in the early hours of the morning, we too slipped into fitful sleep. I woke up to hear the sound of a jeep passing by and woke my friend up to say we should at least hand the sick person to the military for medical help. As we debated about it, we were aware of a deathly stillness. Even the leaves on the trees were still. They seemed to hold their breath. Both of us kept looking at each other and slowly, simultaneously turned our eyes to the friend lying still, motionless. Not a word was said, not a thought spoken. In the silence, we used our pots and pans as shovels and dug a hole; we knew, even without speaking, what we had to do. Hot tears streamed down our faces, mingling with the sweat trickling down our foreheads, and in what seemed to be a fairly deep hole, we buried him. Each of us had our own thoughts. I seemed to remember some of the chants my father said when he officiated a funeral service. I said it in my head, for fear of sounding presumptuous. We waited around the fresh sod for a couple of minutes silently saying our goodbyes, acknowledging the fact that it could have been one of us and without a word moved on. How long we walked in silence I have no idea. But the comradeship we enjoyed during the next few hours will remain unparalleled in my life. Respect and love for each other flooded over us even in our silence. Value of the life of the other and the awareness that life is short and a gift from God reined our minds and hearts. We walked with our heads bowed down in humility knowing that every moment was a gift from God.

Days passed to weeks. Food was scarce; water was nowhere to be found. Even if we found water, it was not drinkable. However, the thirst always took the better of our senses. We would dip our cups in pools or flowing water and take small sips as though small sips would keep the toxicity from affecting us. It was my friend who was beginning to show signs of weariness. One night as we stopped to rest, he implored me to carry on and not delay my journey to be with him. I refused and said we were in this together and I was, at any cost, not leaving him behind. He was too tired to argue. We slept under the tree leaning on the trunk and our shoulders making contact. He soon fell asleep. I stayed awake further into the night, afraid he too might slip away like our other friend. He just got worse and the feeling of death hovering around us was so strong. I began to smell death in every waft of breeze. My friend began to get delirious and was asking me to go on and reach home to talk to his aged parents and convey the messages of love to them. He wanted me to tell them he was happy that he was going. I reassured him that we would soon find help and soon we would be going home together. I tried to keep awake. But tiredness, hunger and mental exhaustion soon drew my eyelids to rest on my cheeks. When I woke up, it was to see the fevered brow of my friend, his parched lips and not a drop of water to wet it. I felt helpless – the kind of helplessness that comes over us when we know what to do but are unable to do it. He took my hand in his and said his goodbye and asked me to go on. That, he said, was the greatest thing I could do for him, while he would lie there believing that I will carry his message to his family. I took one last look at him and moved on, never turning back. My tears flowed like it would never stop. Would his be another decaying, rotting cadaver on the ground, or would someone have the heart, energy and time to bury it? I moved on in my journey alone. Very little hope was left and very little strength. What exactly I did the next few days was of no consequence and nothing important. I trudged on mechanically – with pain trying to overtake tiredness, which in turn was trying to overtake hopelessness. My mind was blank and my brain refused to talk. I was not even capable of self-talk. How many days I walked I have no idea. But there seemed to be more people around me, and there was life beginning to get busy around me gradually, like the break of dawn. I looked around me; more and more people were having lesser fear on their faces. Did this mean I was closer to home? Am I safe/is the war over? Even as relief spread over me, I also felt overwhelming sadness creep in. Why is there no sense of jubilation? I missed my friends – more, the one I had left alongside alive. I found the shade of a tree and sat down to rest my weary feet and body. I lay there, I don't know how long. I was woken up by someone. I opened my eyes and saw it was a soldier. I mumbled something, he nodded and then everything went dark around me. When I woke up, it was in a cool comfortable bed and I was asleep under sheets. Some kind soul had done this; this was an obscure service going on in the corner of the world ... No one would ever know of these acts of kindness, these services. These were the services rendered out of sheer selflessness and for the Glory of the creator. I sat up in bed and was greeted by an old man who smiled with his toothless gum and in a language which he and I alone understood, "Are you ok?" I said I was fine and wanted to be on my way and he agreed. So with the help of that impoverished family, I reached Calcutta and soon was bundled into a train for the next phase of the journey towards home, forgiveness and freedom ... This was going to be a very long journey. The closer I got to home, the longer it seemed to take. The pain and loss of my friends seemed to sink in even more as I was nearing home. What am I to say to the families? That I buried their son? Or that I abandoned their sick son and scurried away to make my escape? Was it possible that my friend, by some spate of luck, was picked up by medical force, treated and already home? Was it possible that my family have accepted me as dead? This was scary ...

Between gratitude for the safety of one's own home,

guilt, sadness and weariness, I reached my own state, familiar landmarks, familiar language and familiar smell of now unfamiliar food. The land of war and hunger seemed like a bad nightmare.

It was the early hours of the morning. Dawn was breaking. The first streaks of light were forcing their way through the night sky, the darkness reluctantly parting to let the light in. I entered the little by-way towards my home. The long driveway (my words) ... led to the house. I could see the house far ahead, silhouetted against the faintly breaking dawn. Memories came flooding in. Anticipation was beating hard in my chest. I could hear the pounding in my ears; it seemed to shut everything else out. What was it going to be like? Who was going to see me first? It probably got to be my father, who always woke up with the breaking dawn for his commune with God. He was a good, devout country parson. Very true and sincere to his calling and his ministry. He had a gentle look and kind eyes. My mother was the epitome of austerity and ruled with an iron hand. I may not even see any softness in her. As these thoughts tumbled over each other and I dragged my feet, I saw someone open the door and come out towards me. She had a lamp in her hand and there were sounds and movements in the house. Lights seem to be lit in every part of the house. My mother hurried her steps and squinting came towards me. "Did I walk towards her or did I wait for her to reach me?" I can't remember, *but one moment I was alone and scared and the next I had the warmth and security of everything that motherhood can bring into your life. I felt hot tears on my hands. Was it from those eyes that had kept the vigil all these years or was it from those eyes that ached with the longing and yearning for home? Perhaps it was both. Soon I had my little sister standing a little far away and watching me with eyes of suspicion and disbelief. My father came out and gently led me to the house. Not a word spoken but volumes passed between us – words of assurance, love and acceptance. I was but a ghost of a figure. Hunger and sickness had driven me to this state. It didn't take my mother long to figure out that I had jaundice. It was no surprise to them or to me. I was just glad to be alive.*

After the marathon of words and narration, undisturbed and pregnant with emotions and truth, he sat there with silent and still eyes staring into the dark. I sat near him, as still as a statue, and in the silence, there passed between us words unsaid but heard, feelings unexpressed but felt, and a closeness which almost bordered on holiness. It would have been sacrilege to say anything. Anything that I said then, I knew, would be inadequate. This story was going to be one that I would turn to many times on this earth before my life is over and I attain my goal.

My father and I shared these intimate moments of soul searching in the most unexpected moments. These moments etched out messages that I would carry in my heart all through my life. It was special because I felt honoured to be let into his inner thoughts and feelings devoid of any pretence. I loved the honesty of his words and the preciseness of his feelings. It helped me mould myself into what I admire in me – my ability to face my thoughts and feelings squarely: To touch reality even as I walk on the edge of unreality; bear the yoke knowing I will be bent but never broken. That night before I retired to bed, I made a decision not to let anything or anyone deter my growth or faith. One message came out clear through his entire narration, to go for what I believe in, to stand up for what I was convinced about. These memories make him real and these words will immortalize him.

Testimonials

I am a fifth generation "Circus Family" and I wouldn't have it any other way! Born in Sarasota, FL, I travelled to different cities for the first 23 years of my life!

And one of the most vibrant memories I have is having the honour of being one of Ms Manna's students. God put her in my life just when I needed her the most!

My parents were going through a separation at the time and she pushed me to focus on myself, my grades and my future! She was the perfect example of a strong and independent woman! Her kindness, understanding and patience allowed me to excel in my interests which were writing and planning events!

And I cannot imagine what that time would have been for me and my younger brother without her there!

Virginia Torres (Student)

The circus life brings exciting adventures but also challenges, both professional and personal. Whether facing her own struggles or helping her friends with words of wisdom, Manna always demonstrated fortitude and determination. The circus was an entirely new experience for Manna and yet she made it her own – working hard, establishing enduring friendships and enriching young minds. She is one to be admired for her strength of courage and character.

Theresa McLean Norton (Head of Wardrobe)

> *Manna as a teacher was and is a Blessing. She took the education of all the students to heart. Every child was special, and they knew they were cherished, loved and understood.*
>
> *To this day, there are students who look for her to tell her how much she meant to them or to share their achievements with her. As a friend, Manna helped me evolve into a strong woman.*
>
> **Sjana Venson (Head of Purchasing)**

> *Manna's life was never easy. My life was never easy. However, our lives were never uneventful. Manna's faith led her to thrive rather than just survive. I continue to learn valuable life lessons from my lifetime friend Manna.*
>
> **Paul Andziewicz (Life-time Friend)**

> *My best memory of you as a teacher is when you took us to that Indian restaurant and introduced us to some of your Indian food! The owner took us to the kitchen to show the tandoor. The food was yummy and I remember everyone having such a good time with you that day. The two lessons I have learnt from you are about being "responsible" and "accountable" for our deeds.*
>
> **Richard Zsilak (Student)**

To describe Manna in a few words is an impossible task. In a nutshell, she is sincere, hard working, compassionate and loving, both as a teacher and friend. We became instant friends, which grew into a lasting friendship. Her outstanding qualities are being highly responsible and taking her job very seriously. She appreciates differences and treats everyone with respect. The parents trusted her without hesitation. She was the best influencer and someone you would want to emulate. We have shared laughter, margaritas and tears.

Elyana (Department of Transportation)

You were one of the best teachers I have ever had. You cared about each and every one of your students as if we were all your own. The train rides with you and the yummy Indian food are among my favourite memories. You are such a beautiful soul and I am beyond thankful to you for being such a huge part of my life. People from the circus never end up just being friends; you have always been more like family to me and my siblings and I appreciate every single bit of it. Teachers like you only happen once every blue moon, and I was lucky enough to have you as mine.

Lexie Marie (Student)

> *I enjoyed having you as a teacher. I loved how you were involved with all the children. Even for Zoë and the others who were around preschool age at that time, you were able to have the older children come up with fun projects for the little kids to do. It was great to have all the children participating together. I always smile whenever I see or think about the picture from then.*
>
> **Becky Lee (Head of Day Care)**